WILLIE PARK JUNIOR was the champion golfer of his time. Born in Musselburgh in 1864, he was the son of Willie Park and nephew of Mungo Park, both Open Championship winners. He won the Open himself twice, in 1887 and 1889. Not only did he participate in challenge matches and demonstrations in Britain, Western Europe and North America, he was also the founder of an international clubmaking company, and he made and sold clubs and balls in many cities. He designed over 160 golf courses worldwide – including over 40 in the United States and 20 in Canada. He wrote the first professional golf book, *The Game of Golf*, in 1886, which he followed in 1920 with *The Art of Putting*. He died an untimely death in 1925.

WALTER STEPHEN worked by night as a baker in Musselburgh in the 1950s, leaving him free to play golf by day over the local course, the Musselburgh Old Course – the oldest golf links still in play in the world. Steeped in the achievements of The Musselburgh School who took golf to the world, he compensates for his own modest performance by celebrating those earlier heroes.

PAUL LAWRIE was born in Aberdeen and is thus the latest Scot to win The Open Championship, which he did in dramatic style in 1999. His achievement comes into perspective when we realise that, of the 29 majors played since then, not one has been won by a European.

The Game of Golf

WILLIE PARK JUNIOR

Luath Press Limited

EDINBURGH

www.luath.co.uk

First published by Longmans, Green, and Co., London, 1896
This edition 2006

ISBN (10): 1-905222-65-3
ISBN (13): 978-1-90522265-0

The paper used in this book is recyclable. It is made from
low chlorine pulps produced in a low energy, low emission
manner from renewable forests.

Printed and bound by
Creative Print and Design, Ebbw Vale

Typeset in 10.5 point Sabon

Contents

List of Illustrations

Foreword

THE MODERN GOLF professional owes a great debt to Willie Park Junior. As well as being one of the best golfers of his generation – probably second only to Vardon – he was a shining example of keenness and enthusiasm. He built up the family club- and ball-making business, every year bringing out a new club or an improved ball. As his golfing prowess faded he developed a new career, designing and building golf courses – over a hundred in the British Isles and Western Europe, forty in the usa and twenty in Canada. Truly he was 'The Man who took Golf to the World'.

He was serious and responsible and could mix at all levels of society – making him the first of a new breed of professionals who replaced the earlier colourful but erratic characters in the game. Their spoken language was blunt and picturesque, but Willie Park went away beyond them to write the first book about golf by a professional golfer.

The Game of Golf (1896) was like Willie himself. It is a serious book of instruction, with no couthy tales or traditions of 'our famous links'. It is solid and reliable. It pioneered photographs and sketches as means of showing the right and wrong ways of mastering the techniques of our great game. Practically every book on golf since his time has copied his basic format. After over a century it can still be read with profit by today's golfer.

I commend this milestone of a book to the notice of every lover of our wonderful game.

Paul Lawrie
October 2006

'The Man in the White Suit' – Willie Park (left) and Harry Vardon posing before their challenge match at North Berwick, 1899.

Introduction

1896 WAS A GOOD year for William Park. Although, at 32, he was no longer a young man, he was clearly still on the way up. By any standards, Willie Park Junior, as we usually refer to him, was a phenomenon and in 1896 his greatness was beginning to emerge. His victories in the Open Championship in 1887 and 1889 were not far behind him and he was still playing well enough in challenge and exhibition matches to make another Open victory likely. The family club- and ball-making business he had virtually taken over was thriving and he was turning out a new club or improved ball every year. Branches were opened in Edinburgh (1891), London and Manchester (1894).

Since he had returned to Musselburgh from Tynemouth at the age of twenty, because of his father's ill-health, he had had enough profitable employment not to have to take up a post as a club professional. Instead he was able to pursue a career which combined competitive play with business management and innovation. His father had agreed to lay out a new golf course at Innerleithen. Willie took over the commitment, surveyed the ground and laid out his proposals on successive Saturday afternoons – without charging a fee, asking only that members would remember William Park and Son when they were buying their clubs.

There followed a stream of commissions as Willie Park laid out new golf courses and improved existing ones, initially in south-east Scotland, and then further afield. In 1895 he made his first visit to America, establishing a branch in New York. He returned in 1896, playing exhibition and challenge matches, memorably against Willie Campbell, of whom more later.

If we think of Willie Park Junior as 'The Man who took Golf to the World', as a golf missionary, setting up new courses, supplying good tools for the job, and teaching and demonstrating to individuals the best way to play, the next step was obvious. He wrote and published in 1896 *The Game of Golf*, the first book about the game written by a professional golfer. This was a milestone in the history of the game and from it one can build up a picture of the game at a time of flux. The book was revolutionary in at least two ways. It meant that anyone who could read English could learn about the game and how to play it from an expert. While it would certainly help to go to a golf course and have 'hands-on' tuition from a professional; with Willie Park's book one could do a great deal oneself, anywhere in the world. One could be learning while he was sleeping.

As its first reviewer said:

> In this book we find a serious contribution to the growing bulk of Golf literature by one of our leading professionals, himself twice Champion, the bearer of an illustrious name in Golf with a playing style that comes down to us as an example of the elegance and grace of the classic Musselburgh school. A careful perusal of its pages shows the reader that here we have the benefit of many years' close application to practice, with the lessons of golfing experience gathered from a lifetime spent at the game, on all sorts of greens and amid all sorts of players.

The 19th century professional golfer was a mixed blessing. The job was a mixture of teacher, player, greenkeeper and caddie, with variable rewards and abundant opportunity for erratic and outrageous behaviour. While 'toffs and serfs' often seem to get on well together, the relationship depends on the skills of the latter. When the skills fade, the erstwhile friends move on. The Victorian professional was skilful, could teach the game, and often had a salty wit – but he could let himself down in company! Willie Park changed that.

He could do anything Andra Kirkaldy – for example – could do, but he could do it in a calm and respectful style.

Photographs often show him in a white suit, thoughtfully studying his opponent preparing to putt. Off the course he was the businessman, with the waistcoat, gold watch and chain. Bob Ferguson (still the only golfer to win the Open three times in succession) had two daughters who worked in the paper mill. Willie's daughter, Doris, had to work for a living, but trained and worked as a masseuse before she married. Above all, by writing *The Game of Golf*, Willie demonstrated that a professional was more than just a good player, he could hold his head up in the presence of millionaires and minor royalty.

Musselburgh in the second half of the 19th century was a real 'hotbed of golfing genius'. It produced five Open Champions: only St Andrews has produced more. (Old) Willie Park won the very first Open in 1860, and three more. In a typical piece of entrepreneurship, a month before *The Game of Golf* was published:

> a full-length portrait of old Willie' was 'painted for his equally celebrated son. Artist proof copies of this picture, handsomely mounted, are obtainable at £3;3s, India prints £2;2s, and ordinary prints £1;1s. Orders for the picture can be left at Park's shop, 115 Cannon Street. (London)

(Old) Mungo, Old Willie's brother, spent his early life at sea, returning to Musselburgh at thirty-five, to win the first Open held there, in 1874. (Young) Willie was twice Open Champion and felt cheated that he did not win in 1898. Bob Ferguson we have met. David ('Deacon') Brown won in 1886.

In addition there was a stream of eager young men (and at least one woman) who ventured forth to take golf to the world. Of these, the most interesting was probably Willie Campbell, said to be 'The World's Best Match Player'. In a life of only 38 years he packed in dozens of exciting matches, often lost through his own hotheadedness. Settled in Boston, he was a main opponent of Willie on his US tours. His wife Georgina, herself a Musselburgh lassie, became the first woman professional in the United States '(and, quite probably, the world)'.

Plain, no nonsense. As was the man, so is the book. Satisfyingly chunky with good stiff covers, it lies reassuringly in the hand. The cover shows a slim bag of clubs leaning on a sand-box; beside it is a fresh white ball. In the distance a flag waves. *The Game of Golf* – the title tells one what it is, no Art of Golf, no pretensions to becoming a champion, no philosophy. Willie does not refer to 'our famous links', nor to the past and present heroes of the game, except to illustrate a point. Willie lays it on the line in his Preface, where he says his book is 'intended for a book of instruction'. Also in the Preface he states his position on lady golfers in an early blow for equality of opportunity – 'There is but one game of golf, and what has been written is applicable to all who play it'.

The anonymous reviewer in *Golf: A Weekly Record of 'Ye Royal and Ancient' Game*, the issue of 1 May 1896, was not too happy about this;

> If one were disposed to find a small fault with the book, it would be that it is too serious. It has none of the lightness of touch and humour presented by the pens of Mr Hutchinson and Sir Walter Simpson; and now and again we could wish to hear a good story to point a moral, for, of these we should imagine Willie Park has heard and enjoyed hundreds.'

The reviewer missed the point; Hutchinson and Simpson were amateurs, Willie was a professional.

The book is remarkable for its wealth of illustrations. The photographs are reproduced well by a new cheap process appropriate for a book selling at 7/6d (37.5 pence). Willie himself modelled for most of the photographs but JE Laidlay, a top amateur, was also used for photographs and sketches of e.g. feet positions. The book was intended for amateurs to read, so an amateur role model was desirable.

Laidlay was a top golfer in his time – Amateur Champion 1889, 1891, runner-up three times. Open 1893, runner-up. Played for Scotland every year 1902-11 (when he was fifty-one). He held the Musselburgh course record of 72, 1876-92.

It was Laidlay who pioneered the so-called Vardon grip. He took 6 wickets for Scotland against Yorkshire at their strongest. He was a pioneer of wildlife photography, carved beautiful furniture and was clearly the complete amateur.

Mr Laidlay is used to show how a degree of variation is permissible and how a man's stance can alter over the years and still be effective. (Willie may seem to be inconsistent here. Above he says there is only one game of golf, now he is admitting that a degree of deviation is acceptable).

Chapter 1 is a basic introduction to the game, its language, its rules and methods of play. If it seems simple and straightforward to us today this is because the writing is so plain and clear and because we have had a hundred years of later books (to say nothing of film and video) quoting and restating the essential truths WPJ is laying down in this chapter. He welcomes the dissimilarity of golf courses as one of the chief pleasures of the game. Hazards, he says, are there to catch topped balls and to trap balls played too much on either side. Competitions are explained, 'bogey' defined and details of scoring clarified.

Going on to clubs and balls he describes the manufacture and characteristics of the main clubs, giving the not disinterested advice that we should: 'if it be at all possible, buy direct from the maker'. A page and a half are given over to the development and virtues of 'the bulger' – Park's own manufacture. Without being over-strenuous in his argument he must have convinced many a player that he must have this club.

Incidental comments give us a feeling for the times and enable us to make comparisons with our own era. Thus: 'Experience proves that 200 yards is about the average limit of really long driving'. (Twenty-five years later, Willie drew up plans for a course at Castine, Maine which demonstrated that – post-Haskell – he now considered 240 yards a good drive).

The general condition of courses in his time can be guessed at from his advice to carry a spare driver and brassie, in case a club was broken, and, 'with regard to balls, it is a safe plan never to take out fewer than half a dozen'.

The Long Game, Approaching, Putting and Play Out of Hazards are each covered in some detail. Effective diagrams illustrate the position of the feet: dancing manuals developed this illustrative technique further. Again, interesting changes can be deduced, as in the use of sand to make a good tee (or a bad one, if one is stupid enough). The stymie is illustrated and discussed on four pages.

As the *Golf* reviewer said:

> The practical chapters... are fascinating reading, illustrated as all the points are by reproductions of Park's own positions and grip.

Older golfers today, who recall the stymie, rage and grate their teeth at its unfairness and become almost apoplectic at the suggestion that its reintroduction would liven up the game around the greens. Willie, characteristically, does not discuss morality, nor rail against Fate. With Presbyterian acceptance, he gets right down to the business of – how do you play the stymie? In summary, go over or screw it round. 'Both methods are equally good, if successful' – a statement which could mean everything, or nothing. Imagine practising stymies! And the delicacy of touch required! Yet that is what WPJ advocates, while admitting that 'the chief requisite is nerve'.

Modern books on golf are unlikely to have a chapter on Laying Out and Keeping Golf-Links. This is of great interest because Willie Park was eventually involved with over 160 courses, most of them designed from scratch. By the time his book was written he was able to point out that many courses had been created in conditions far removed from the ideal, the seaside links. Old pasture or moorland was perfectly suitable, but good arable land sown with good grass seed took longer to settle down to a satisfactory state. He reminds us that all good courses have, to a certain degree, evolved: but that, for a new course, an architect with some experience is necessary. Again, a little self-promotion! A course with nine good holes is to be preferred to one with eighteen unsatisfactory ones.

When it comes to planning, one must lay out the tees and

greens first. The first tee and last green should be near the clubhouse and a bird's eye view should help to locate the others, which should be marked by stakes. Details of the layout will depend on the natural character of the ground. 'Par play should require about eighty strokes'.

Nine holes out and nine holes back are advocated but WPJ was forced to build many courses where the available ground made this impossible. At times he laid out courses with two circuits of nine holes ending at the clubhouse, making for more variety in play. He was against 'cross holes' but felt obliged to use them when acreage was limited. Parallel fairways should not be too close, for obvious safety reasons.

The first few holes should be fairly long and 'easy of play', so that players can get away quickly, or 'get squandered' as the old Musselburgh caddie said. Thus they can get nicely warmed up. There should be variation in the length of the holes and Park goes into some detail on this. Putting greens get full consideration. They should be as large as possible, not flat, but gently undulating.

All hazards should be visible to the golfer at his stance. (The editor still feels sore at WPJ's lapse at the sixth at Forres.) By placing bunkers round the green at 4, 8 and 11 o'clock, Park left a clear road for running the ball up on to the green, believing this to be more skilful than lofting with an iron. Erratic play should always be met with punishment.

Even course upkeep is dealt with. Sheep are good for keeping down the grass and enrich the course. Cattle and horses are not welcome. In 1896 Willie Park saw the need for mechanical grass control.

Forty-five pages were devoted to The Laws of Golf, which were very much of an issue at the time. Many clubs had their own variations and Willie Park printed the rules of the R and A and Royal Wimbledon, with a table showing the differences and his own observations. After a number of pronouncements and codes of rules, by 1901 the R and A and its rules were generally accepted but were not adequate for all circumstances. Not till 1919 could it be said that all ambiguities and alternatives had been ironed out and the R and A could assume its present controlling authority.

By way of summary, the *Golf* review cannot be bettered:

> The book is handsomely got up, it is written with concise vigour and fullness of knowledge. The book is one which ought to be in the hands of every golfer and on the table of every club.

There once was a man who went to a performance of Hamlet, only to complain that the work was full of quotations. Similarly, today's reader might find *The Game of Golf* staid and straightforward, lacking in colour and novelty. Because it was the first it cannot match the style and colour of the hundreds of successors which copied it. Yet, in our 21st century, it is still worth reading to confirm how the essentials of the game are unchanging. Most of WPJ's advice is still good advice and it is clearly and concisely expressed.

Walter Stephen
October 2006

WILLIAM PARK, JUN.

CHAMPION GOLFER, 1887-89

WITH NUMEROUS ILLUSTRATIONS

FIFTH IMPRESSION

LONGMANS, GREEN, AND CO.

39 PATERNOSTER ROW, LONDON

NEW YORK AND BOMBAY

1901

Frontispiece from original version of *The Game of Golf*

Preface

ALTHOUGH PROFESSIONAL GOLFERS have always been teachers of the game, their instruction has been imparted more by example than by precept. Such a method was and is undoubtedly the best, but it is not available to the same extent at the present day as it was, say, fifty or even twenty years ago, and hence a demand has sprung up for books of instruction. Amateur golfers have hitherto been the sole contributors to the literature of the game, but the belief has frequently been expressed to me that a volume coming from a professional would be read with interest, and it has also been suggested that I should undertake to write one. Encouraged by such friendly remarks, the attempt has been made, and it is hoped that what has been written will be of service to golfers. Being intended for a book of instruction, the history of the game is omitted, and no reference is made either to our famous links or to the past and present heroes of the game, save with the view of illustrating the more effectually some of the subjects dealt with. An endeavour has been made to write as concisely and briefly as is consistent with giving intelligible information.

I hope that lady golfers will not feel disappointed because they are not specially referred to. There is but one game of golf, and what has been written is applicable to all who play it. Proof is not wanting that there are lady players inferior to none save a few of the cracks.

I have to thank Mr J E Laidlay for kindly supplying me with photographs and diagrams of the style of play of which he is so able an exponent, and I cannot conclude without acknowledging my indebtedness to Mr John Anderson for the assistance he has given me in preparing this book for the press.

W P, JR
Musselburgh, 1896

CHAPTER ONE

The Game of Golf

ALTHOUGH GOLF HAS become a universal pastime only within the last few years, it is a game of considerable antiquity, and has been played in Scotland from time out of mind. Who invented golf, if indeed it was invented, is not known, and it seems probable that it has been evolved from a game similarly played, but in a crude form, rather than invented. At one time it would appear to have been the prevailing form of sport in Scotland, and so far back as the year 1457 there is an Act of the Scottish Parliament prohibiting it as interfering with the practice of archery, then all important as a martial exercise and a means of national defence. A few of the older golf clubs have records dating back more than a century, some of which seem to point to the fact that the clubs had been in existence at prior dates, although the records are now lost. The Honourable the Edinburgh Company of Golfers have minutes dated in 1744; the Royal and Ancient Golf Club of St Andrews dates back to 1754; the Royal Musselburgh Golf Club was instituted in 1774; the first minute-book of the Bruntsfield Links Golf Club dates from 1787; and the Edinburgh Burgess Golfing Society claims to have been instituted in 1735. There is, however, a golf club in England – the Royal Blackheath Golf Club – instituted in 1608, which has, it is believed, more ancient records than any of the Scottish clubs; but it is doubted whether some of the clubs first mentioned are not older in point of fact, although actual proof of this cannot be produced. Whether the Scottish clubs are more ancient or not, the Blackheath Club has the honour not only of possessing the oldest records, but also of being one of the very few golf clubs in England until within a comparatively recent period.

To describe shortly the game of golf, one may say that it

consists in playing a ball, with the smallest number of strokes, from certain places called teeing-grounds into holes made for the purpose at considerable distances away. This is but a rough and ready description of the game, but it may serve as a general introduction, and tend to a better understanding of the more particular explanations contained in the succeeding pages.

The ground upon which the play takes place is called a 'links' or 'golf-course' or 'golf-green.' When the latter terms are employed, the adjective is commonly omitted, and 'the course' or 'the green' alone used. The word 'green' is apt to be somewhat puzzling to novices, because it is frequently applied indiscriminately not only to the whole links, but also to that particular part called 'the putting-green.'

Along the sea-coast there lie large tracts of undulating sandy ground, quite unsuited for agricultural purposes, and covered with short, velvety turf, interspersed with sand-holes, whins, rushes, and benty grass, and it is on these that golf has in the generality of cases been played. Such stretches of ground are in Scotland called links, but that word has now come to be almost exclusively used to signify any ground upon which golf is played. These seaside links are the best adapted for golf, but there are many excellent inland courses laid out upon any land covered with turf which happened to be available.

The extent and form of a golf-course are quite arbitrary, depending in a great measure upon the nature of the ground, which makes it impossible to find two golf-courses exactly alike. This dissimilarity, it may be remarked, is one of the chief pleasures of the game, because a visit to a strange links lends variety, and helps to bring out the judgment and skill of the golfer. Eighteen holes are recognised to be the full number a links should contain, but fifteen, twelve, nine, and even six hole courses are by no means uncommon. The lengths of some of the best-known courses of eighteen holes – adding together the measurements from hole to hole – vary from about two and three-quarter miles to three and three-quarter miles. With regard to the plan on which the holes are laid down, there is no fixed system; on some links the first nine holes follow each other consecutively in an approximately straight line in one direction, and the remaining nine holes return in much the same line in the opposite direction, while on others they are placed irregularly as the ground permits. For instance, at St Andrews, which is considered to be one of the best eighteen-hole greens in the Kingdom, the course has the shape of a shepherd's crook, the players going out to the end of the crook and returning the opposite way; at Musselburgh, which is possibly the best nine-hole links in existence, the shape is something like an irregular oblong, three holes out, one across, four holes back, and one home to the starting-place; at North Berwick and Leven, both eighteen-hole courses, the players go straight out and come back in lines parallel to one another; while at Sandwich, a splendid links, the holes are placed irregularly, something in the form of a capital T. The examples given will convey some idea of the form of a golf-links; but so long as the green is laid out to test good play, the shape is quite immaterial.

At suitable places on the course teeing-grounds are marked off from which the play to each hole begins – the first teeing-ground being the starting-point from which the game commences – and at distances varying from 100 to 500 yards or thereby from these teeing-grounds putting-greens are formed, in which the holes are made into which the ball is to be played. The size of the holes, as fixed by the laws of the game, is four and a quarter inches in diameter, and at least four inches deep, and flags mounted on tall pins are placed in the holes to indicate their positions; such flags must be capable of being lifted out when the players are on the putting-greens. Between the teeing-grounds and the various putting-greens there are, invariably, either natural or artificially formed 'hazards', in the shape of sand-holes (or 'bunkers'), clumps of whins, and rushes or similar obstructions placed for the purpose of entrapping, and so punishing, badly played balls. The hazards sometimes extend right across the line of play, and at other times are to be found on either side thereof, the object being in the first case to catch topped balls (*i.e.* balls struck on the top, causing them to run along the ground instead of rising in the air), and in the second case to trap balls played too much to one side or the other. As the play from hole to hole is continuous, the teeing-ground for the second hole is generally near the first hole, the tee for the third near the second, and so on. The chapter on laying out and keeping golf-links contains fuller information on this subject.

It is a curious fact that there are no written laws of golf regarding the implements – either clubs or balls – to be used in playing the game; but it is safe to assume that only golf-clubs and golf-balls can be used.

The mode of play has already been briefly explained. But there are two methods, viz. 'match play,' in which individuals contend against each other for holes, and 'medal play,' in which any number compete among themselves for scores.

MATCH PLAY – the most genuine form of golf – admits of several variations. The most usual match is *a single* – that is, two individuals play against each other. They start at the first teeing-ground, and each tees his own ball on a small pinch of sand called a 'tee' – sand for the purpose being provided at each teeing-ground. If they cannot agree which is to strike off first, it is usually decided by tossing up a coin. This privilege of playing first from the tee is called 'the honour.' Each player endeavours to drive his ball from the tee on to the putting-green, and to put it into the hole with the smallest number of strokes. The player holing his ball in the fewest strokes wins the hole; if both take the same number, the hole is said to be 'halved' – neither wins it. The game proceeds from teeing-ground to hole until the full eighteen holes, of which it generally consists, have been successively played, or until the match is finished. The player who wins the greater number of holes wins the match; but if both win an equal number the match is said to be halved, or, in other words, is drawn. Except in the case of the tee-shots, the person whose ball is farther from the hole plays before the other. Thus it may happen that one of the couple, on reaching the putting-green, has played two strokes while his opponent may have played three or four, or even more; and it is also possible that one of them may have to take two or three consecutive strokes before his opponent again plays, until he puts his ball nearer the hole than his opponent's is at the time. After the balls have been struck off from the tee, they cannot be touched or moved with anything except the golf-clubs, save in the exceptional cases provided for in the rules, or subject to the penalties therein mentioned.

A good golfer can drive a ball any distance up to, rough-ly speaking, a couple of hundred yards, and when he gets to the putting-green he should be able to put his ball into the hole in two strokes. On reading this, many persons will no doubt think that golf is quite a simple game – and simple it is, in the-ory; moreover, to see golf played by a 'crack' makes it look not only simple but also comparatively easy. But let it be tried, and it will then be found that it is not quite so easy as it looks. A golf-ball is not a large object, being only about an inch and three-quarters in diameter, and to hit it accurately when it lies clear on the green – and accurately hit it must be to make it travel – requires both skill and practice. I have said when it lies clear; but the ball may not lie clear: it may be imbedded in grass, or it may have lodged in a 'cup' or small hollow in the ground, which considerably increases the difficulty of hitting it properly. Apart from mere hitting, the distance and the direction in which the ball is to be driven must be attended to; because, as already pointed out, the hazards are intended and are always so placed as to catch badly played strokes; and if care and skill be not exercised, one is likely to find his ball in a difficult position out of which there may be some trouble in extricating it. In addition to all this, when getting near to the putting-green, or 'approaching', the amount of force requisite to play the ball on to the green and yet not beyond it requires to be judged; and in putting – as playing strokes on the put-ting-green is called – the requisite strength and the proper line of play to send the ball into the hole have to be nicely calcu-lated. But the player who has obtained even a small degree of mastery over the game feels a keen delight in endeavouring to overcome such difficulties; and the same amount of satisfaction as is derived by golfers from well-played strokes is probably not to be found in playing any other game.

In match play it is not usual to count the actual number of strokes taken. Golf has a language of its own. When a golfer plays the same number of strokes as his opponent, he is said to play 'the like.' When both have played the same number they are said to be 'like as they lie.' When the one has played a stroke more than his opponent, he is said to have 'played the odds.' When he plays two or any greater number of strokes more than his opponent, he is said to play 'two more' or 'three more,' as the case may be. Now, suppose one of the couple has played three strokes and the other five strokes – that is, 'two more' – and it is the turn of the former to play, he does not say. 'This is my fourth stroke against your fifth,' but he says, 'I am playing one off two.' Similarly, he may be playing 'one off three,' and so on; of course, when he plays one off two, if he has again to play before his opponent, he then plays the like. In a 'hole game' it is not of the slightest consequence what actual number of strokes is taken; the only object each golfer need have in view is to get his ball into the hole in one stroke less than his opponent. Having played the first hole, if it is won, the person winning it is said to be 'one up,' and his opponent 'one down.' If it be halved, the match is 'all even.' If halved, the player who originally had the honour again drives off first for the second hole. If either party wins the hole the party winning it obtains the honour; and so the game proceeds from hole to hole until the match is finished.

It is not always necessary that the agreed on number of holes should actually be played out to finish the match; Suppose, for example, that one of the players gets to be 'four up,' and there remain but three holes to play, he has won the match, because it must be obvious that even if his opponent were to win all the three remaining holes, the first supposed player would at the end of the round be still one up. In such a case the successful player is said to win his match by four up and three to play. Similarly, he may be two up and one to play, or seven up and six to play, or seven up and five to play, or any such combination. The match originally made (called the long match) being finished a few holes from home, the remaining holes are generally played as a 'bye.' When a player is, say, three holes up on his opponent, and there are only three to be played, that player is said to be 'dormy three,' 'dormy four,' 'dormy five,' etc., applying similarly to the number of holes he is up with the like number remaining to be played. When a player is 'dorm' he cannot lose the game; it may result in a halved match, however, if the opponent succeeds in taking all the remaining holes.

A golf-match is sometimes played by a '*foursome*', and, as the term implies, four persons engage in it, two playing against the other two. The play is in no particular different from that in a single above described, except that, after the tee-shot, each of the two players who are partners take alternate strokes at the ball, and they drive off from the tees alternately.

A *three-ball match* is another variation in which three persons play each his own ball, and the game may be arranged in two ways. First, each person may play against each of the other two, counting in the usual manner. Such an arrangement does not, however, make a very good match – not so good as a single – and it is somewhat troublesome to keep a note of the state of the game, as, of three players (who may be called A, B, and C, for the purpose of illustrating what I mean), A may be two up with B and three down with C, while B is one up with C; and besides all this, it is a three-sided match, and the adage about three being no company applies in golf as in other things. The second mode of arranging a three-ball match is for one person to play against the 'best ball' of the other two; that is to say: Suppose A, B, and C play a three-ball match, in which A plays against the best ball of B and C: if A takes five strokes to a hole, while B and C each take six, A would win that hole; but if A takes five strokes, while either B or C also takes five and the other takes six or seven or any greater number, the hole would be halved: and again, if A as before takes five strokes, and either B or C takes only four, while the other takes more, then A would lose the hole. It will thus be seen that A plays against whichever of B and C takes the fewest strokes at any hole. This makes a capital match, if, in the case supposed, A is a considerably better player than both B and C. In a three-ball match of this description there are only two sides, and it is a hard match for the single ball to win, because the other side has two chances against his one.

Four-ball matches are sometimes, but not very frequently, played; and in them sides are chosen, two balls playing against the other two, and the best ball on each side counting.

It is not always the case that a golfer can find an opponent of his own calibre, and when a good and an inferior player make a match, it is usual for the good player to give to the other 'odds,' depending upon their respective merits. This may be done in two ways – first, by allowing him a certain number of holes of start, which they arrange between themselves. For example, A, a good player, makes a match with B, an inferior player, and allows him say five holes of a start; unless A beats B (counting *actual* play) by more than five holes he loses the match; if he beats him by five holes (counting *actual* play) the match is halved, B having that allowance; if A beats B by four holes (counting *actual* play), B wins the match by one hole, in virtue of his allowance; but, on the other hand, if A finishes six up (counting *actual* play), then he (A) wins the match by one hole. The second method of giving odds is by giving strokes at certain holes to the inferior player. Thus A may allow B 'a stroke a hole,' that is to say, B's second at each hole will count as his first, and his third as his second, and so on; or the allowance may be a stroke at every alternate hole, which is called giving 'half one'; or it may be a stroke at every third hole, giving a 'third' – or any variation of this nature. Handicapping is more fully dealt with in the chapter devoted to that subject.

It will readily be understood that if club competitions were conducted on the lines of match play it would not be possible, when a large number of competitors enter, to finish the competition in less than three or four days. The competitors would require to be drawn against each other, and to play successive rounds of the links until, by a process of survival of the fittest, the ultimate winner vanquished all his opponents. To obviate this, club competitions, with the exception of club tournaments, are usually played under MEDAL RULES. In medal play it matters not how many or how few competitors there are, as each individual player counts the number of strokes he takes to each hole, and the total for the eighteen holes forms his score. The player having the lowest score, either actual or after deduction of a handicap, is the winner of the competition.

'BOGEY' COMPETITIONS – An innovation in competitions has recently been made by each competitor playing against what is termed a 'Bogey' score. The method of play is as follows: The committee in charge of the competition fix a fictitious score for each hole, say four strokes for the first hole, six for the second, five for the third, and so on. This 'Bogey' score usually represents par play over the green, and it is made known before the competition begins, so that each competitor knows what he has to do at every hole. Each player counts his score at every hole, and if he holes out at that particular hole in fewer strokes, or in the same number, or in more than the appointed number, he wins, halves, or loses the hole to 'Bogey,' as the case may be. At the end of the game the number of holes won from 'Bogey' are placed against those lost to 'Bogey,' and the player who is the greatest number of holes up or the fewest down wins the competition.

In competitions for prizes ties are invariably played off by the parties who have tied. In ties under 'Bogey' play the cards of the competitors who tie may, however, be compared against each other, and the one who is up on the others declared the winner. But this can only be done with fairness when these competitors have actually played out every hole.

The rule before stated in regard to the ball farther from the hole being played first, and as to the honour, ought to be strictly observed both in match and medal play, subject, as regards the latter, to the special rule for medal play § (9). Although in medal competitions holes are not won or lost as in match play, the honour is invariably accorded to him who takes the fewest actual strokes to the previous hole.

MATCHES BETWEEN GOLF CLUBS or Golf Societies are frequently played. In these each club selects from its best players a team of a certain number agreed on beforehand, and arranges the players of the team in their order of merit, the best players being placed at the top of the list. The player first on the list of the one team is matched against the player first on the list of the other team, and so on. Each couple plays the full number of holes, and at the end of the play each team counts up the number of holes by which its individual members have beat their opponents, and the club whose team has the largest number of holes to its credit is the winner.

It may be noticed that the OPEN GOLF CHAMPIONSHIP is played under Medal Rules. At present the play extends over two days, thirty-six holes being played each day, and the player with the lowest aggregate score is the winner. On the other hand, the AMATEUR GOLF CHAMPIONSHIP is played by matches. If the number of entrants be not such as will result in their being ultimately reduced to one, without byes at the later stages of the game, a sufficient number of byes is drawn at first to attain this object. The competitors are in the first stage drawn in couples, the defeated player of each couple being forced to retire at the finish of each stage, and the successful player of couple number one engaging the successful player of couple number two, and so on in successive stages until only one player remains, who is the amateur champion for the year.

CLUB TOURNAMENTS by matches are played on lines similar to the Amateur Championship, the only difference being that between each stage a week or more is usually allowed to elapse, so as to give the competitors ample time to play off their matches without inconvenience.

CHAPTER TWO

Golf Clubs and Balls

Golf Clubs

THE FIRST DIFFICULTY that presents itself to any one who desires to learn to play the game of golf is the choice of clubs and balls. In the older days this was a much simpler matter than it is now: the number of clubs was then limited; there was a plentiful supply of good material for their manufacture, and there were only a few makers, all of whom had a thorough knowledge of their business. It was therefore unlikely that a purchaser, however little knowledge he had of the subject, would be put in possession of worthless clubs. He had only to go to any clubmaker, state what he desired – the extent of his purchase being regulated by the length of his purse – and he was tolerably certain of getting good value for his money. Nowadays all this is entirely changed. Clubs are placed on the market by numberless makers, many of whom have but a limited knowledge of the game or of what is required to play it properly; good, well-seasoned wood is difficult to get, and is expensive, so that temptations are placed in the way of makers to manufacture clubs out of inferior material. Numberless patent clubs, many of them contrived more to create than to supply wants, and other so-called requisites for the game, are put into the hands of the inexperienced, rendering it more difficult now than formerly for those who are beginning to play golf to get a really serviceable set of clubs. The best recommendation that can be given is – see that only clubs of some maker of standing and reputation are obtained, and, if it be at all possible, buy direct from the maker. Sometimes clubs are offered for sale at prices considerably lower than what clubmakers usually charge, but one ought not to allow himself to be led

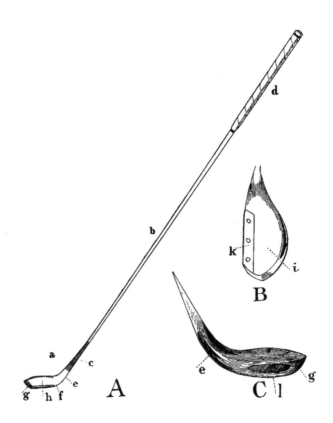

FIG I – A WOODEN CLUB

A, the whole club; B, the 'sole'; C, back view of the head; a, the
head; b, the shaft; c, the 'scare', or part where head and shaft are
fastened and bound together; d, the leather grip or handle; e, the
neck; f, the heel; g, the toe or nose; h, the face; i, the sole; k, the
bone; l, the lead.

away by the idea of getting a cheaper article. It is not possible to produce a really good, well-finished club for a less price than that now charged by the best makers; and it must be borne in mind that in clubs, possibly more than in anything else, the cheapest may in the end be the dearest. A practised eye and hand can have little difficulty in selecting a good club, but to the inexperienced all clubs seem more or less the same. It is the skill in selecting and shaping the wood, and the workmanship in putting together the parts, that make the difference between good and bad.

The illustrations, Figs. 1 and 2, show the different parts of a wooden and an iron club.

After giving a list of the clubs ordinarily used, and describing the various purposes for which they are intended, some hints will be given with the view of aiding in their selection.

The principal clubs are the following, viz.: Driver, Brassyniblick, Putter, Cleek, Iron, Mashie, and Iron-niblick. Of these the first three are made entirely of wood – wooden clubs – and the remainder have iron heads – iron clubs.

Besides those enumerated in the foregoing list, the following clubs are frequently used; and, though not generally forming part of the indispensable equipment of a golfer, one or more of them is usually to be found included in a set. They are: Spoons, Driving-cleek, Driving-mashie, Putting-cleek, Putting-iron, and metal Putter, Driving-putter, Driving-iron, and Lofting-iron. All of these, except the Spoons and Driving-putter, have iron or metal heads.

Until about ten years ago all clubs were made with straight faces, although no doubt they were sometimes made with more or less hook to suit the fancy of players. In the year 1884 the idea occurred to me of trying a club with a convex instead of the usual straight face, and having made such a club, I played with it during that and the subsequent years – in fact, I played with it at the Open Championship of 1885. It may be of interest if the principle of this club, which from its shape has been named 'the bulger,' is shortly explained. In playing with straight-faced clubs it is found that if the ball be struck

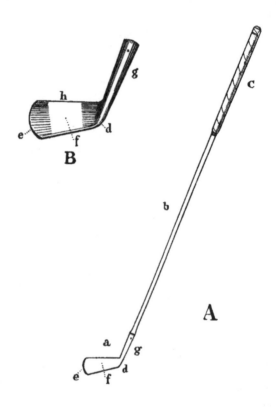

FIG. 2 – AN IRON CLUB

A, the whole club; *B*, the head – front view; *a*, the head; *b*, the shaft; *c*, the leather grip or handle; *d*, the heel; *e*, the toe or nose; *f*, the face; *g*, the socket or hose; *h*, the blade.

with the heel of the club it will fly, not in a straight line, but curving towards the right of the player; while if struck with the toe of the club it will curve towards the left. The convex face of the bulger is intended to counteract the effect of hitting off the heel or toe, and ensure straight flight. It must be kept in mind, however, that the bulger does not counteract deviation in flight caused by slicing or pulling, and indeed, a ball sliced with a bulger will travel with far more curve than if sliced with a straight-faced club. As time has gone on it has been found desirable to somewhat modify the shape of the heads, which are now made with rather less convexity or bulge than was customary a few years ago. Bulgers have been received by golfers with great favour, and their popularity has gone on increasing by leaps and bounds; they have very largely supplanted straight-faced clubs, and it is hardly possible to cite better evidence than this as to their good qualities. All wooden driving-clubs – drivers, spoons, brassy-spoons, and brassy-niblicks – are now usually made with bulger heads; but bulger putters, although occasionally made, are less frequently seen, and are, in fact, seldom used. The bulger principle is as yet practically confined to wooden clubs; for although bulger cleeks and irons have been made, they are not in general use, and do not appear to meet with the approval of players.

Patent golf-clubs have been mentioned, and it is proposed to refer to such of them as may be considered necessary or desirable as occasion requires. To give a complete list would be impossible, as each day sees the birth of some new patent; and to describe the various clubs which have been patented, and their intended uses, would require a large volume devoted to that subject alone.

No one, not even he who has just heard the word golf pronounced, will ever for a moment imagine that all the clubs before enumerated are identical in character. As a matter of fact, they are very different; and while it is not possible to lay down strictly and definitely the exact purpose or stroke for which each must be used – this depending greatly upon the skill of the player – I will endeavour to state the primary object

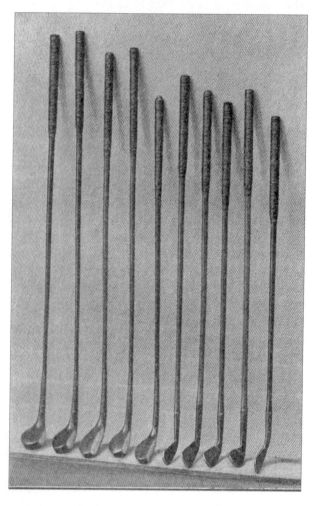

FIG. 3 – MODERN GOLF CLUBS

for which each is intended. Fig. 3 shows a group of modern clubs, and an idea of the differences in their make may be obtained therefrom. The clubs shown are: Bulger Driver, Straight-faced Driver, Spoon, Brassy-niblick, Putter, Cleek, Iron, Mashie, Iron-niblick, and Park's Patent Putter. As the simplest method of explaining such differences, the clubs are dealt with categorically in the order in which they are above mentioned.

The Driver, or play club as it is frequently called, is the most powerful club of a set, and should have a fine springy shaft, adapted in length to suit the player, and should have little or no loft on the face (*i.e.* the face should be almost perpendicular when the club-head is laid on the ground); consequently with it the ball can be driven a greater distance than with any other club. It is therefore used for the first strokes at each hole – the tee-strokes – and also for playing through the green, where the ball lies clear enough to admit of its being used, and when the distance to the hole makes it an advantage to drive the ball as far as possible.

The Brassy-niblick is made with a much smaller head than the driver. It has the face considerably 'spooned' (or sloped back from the bone to the top of the head) with the object of raising the ball in the air, and the sole is shod with a brass plate. The shaft is generally rather less supple than in the driver. It is used largely for playing through the green when the driver cannot be taken, and for playing out of small shallow holes or cups it has no equal, the small head allowing it to pick up the ball better than any other club. Brassies – as all clubs shod with metal are usually and briefly termed – are really of modern invention. The brassy was first used on Musselburgh Links. As many readers will know, its southern boundary is the highroad from Edinburgh to Haddington, and a ball driven on to the road had to be played as it lay. Being a hard macadamised road, playing off it with a wooden club – and in these days there were few iron clubs – frequently entailed the rather severe penalty of a broken club-head, and the genius of a certain gentleman, whose ball got on to the road with great regularity, suggested the brass plate, which was found to successfully answer the purpose of preserving the club-head from injury. Brassies are therefore well adapted for playing a ball off a hard bottom, where an ordinary wooden club would be liable to fracture.

The Putter, as its name indicates, is intended for putting, or playing short strokes on the putting-green. This club is the shortest of all in the shaft, and it is more upright – in fact, the shaft is little more than at right angles to the plane of the head. The head is heavier, and the shaft very stiff; it should have none of that perceptible suppleness which distinguishes the shafts of all the other wooden clubs. It has been said that the head and shaft lie at little more than right angles to each other; in the more modern putters the angle is greater, or, as it is technically expressed, the head is flatter. This is a matter depending entirely upon the taste of the individual player.

The Cleek among iron clubs is what the driver is among wooden clubs. It is the longest of all iron clubs in the shaft, though not so long as a driver, and the blade has least loft, or pitch, as it is more frequently termed when speaking of cleeks. A cleek will thus drive further than any other iron club.

The Iron is deeper in the blade than is the cleek, and has more loft. It will not drive so far as the cleek, but throws the ball higher into the air. This is the club most generally used for playing approaches.

The Mashie is comparatively a modern club. It is shorter in the blade than the iron and has rather more loft, while it is larger than the niblick and has rather less loft, being in fact a compromise between the two. It is mostly used for short approaches, and for playing the ball out of whins and difficulties. Mashies are made in various ways: some have round noses and some square; in the former case they are called mashie-niblicks – the latter are, however, the more useful for general all-round work. In playing approaches with this club few golfers take a full stroke, more usually limiting it to a half, or, at most, a three-quarter swing.

The Niblick is used almost exclusively for bunkers and

hazards, and is undoubtedly the best club for this kind of play. The head is small and round, not much larger than the ball. For bunkers it has no equal; but if it is intended to strike *the ball*, should it lie clear enough in a hazard, the hitting requires to be somewhat accurate, because the head is so small there is a danger of hitting with the heel.

Spoons are divided into long, mid, and short. The head of the spoon is the same as that of the driver, but the face is made with just about the same degree of loft as a brassy, and the shaft is similarly stiff. The words long, mid, and short refer to the length of shaft, and may also be taken to be indicative of the distance the various spoons will drive, as it is of course possible, other things being equal, to drive further with a club having a long shaft than with one having a shorter. Spoons are almost entirely superseded by brassies and cleeks, but they are still sometimes used for strokes where it is an advantage to drive the ball higher in the air than can be done with a play club. Spoons are occasionally shod with brass on the sole, in which case they are called brassy-spoons. In addition to those above-mentioned, golfers of bygone days used a 'baffy' (or baffing) spoon, which was a modification of the short-spoon with a very stiff shaft and a strong head, having the face very much lofted. With the baffy all strokes approaching the hole used to be played. Instead of hitting the ball 'clean,' the stroke was baffed, that is to say, the head of the spoon was made to strike between the ball and the ground, the result being that a back spin was imparted to the ball which lessened the amount of run after alighting on the putting-green. Nowadays the iron has taken the place of this club. To many who remember the brilliant way in which golfers whose names are historic handled these spoons, their disappearance is a matter of regret; but it is to be feared that the iron age of golf has doomed them, and that they will soon be known only as relics of the past.

Of the Driving-cleek there are many forms. The plain driving-cleek is just an ordinary cleek, with less loft than usual on the face and a longer shaft, the spring of it being suited to the weight of the head. Various patent driving-cleeks are to be obtained – one is a patent of my own. My patent was, I believe, the first to come out. The general principle is the weighting of the blade of the cleek behind the point of impact with the ball, and all driving-cleeks are made more or less on this principle or a modification of it. There is no doubt that these cleeks enable a longer ball to be driven than can be done with an ordinary cleek; but of course the best club for driving is a driver. When, however, a ball is lying badly, and it is not possible to pick it up with a wooden club, a driving-cleek is of use, as it will get away a longer stroke than is possible with an ordinary cleek.

Driving-mashies may be said to be modifications of driving-cleeks; the mashie-shaped head is retained, but made with more or less pitch – frequently with almost none – to suit the tastes of various players. They are very useful clubs on heavy greens, as the small head is well adapted for making the best of a bad-lying ball.

Putting-cleeks and irons and metal putters are all intended to be used in place of wooden putters. Some players maintain that the ball can be made to run straighter and truer off iron than off wood, but this is, I think, a matter of taste as much as anything else. The supposed distinction between putting-cleeks and irons and metal putters is that the cleeks usually have some loft on the face, while the latter are deeper in the face and have no loft at all. This want of loft is, in my opinion, rather a disadvantage than otherwise, because, unless there is loft, the club is apt, under certain conditions, to make the ball jump, and it need hardly be said that this is fatal to good putting. Putting being one of the most important parts of the game, if not the most important, a great deal of attention has been directed to perfecting this club, and several makers have taken out patents for improvements on it. Among others, I have endeavoured to improve the ordinary putter, and hold a patent for a putting-cleek of my own invention. This cleek has a bend in the neck just above the blade; it is shown in the group of clubs, Fig. 3. The idea occurred during practice for a tournament, when I happened to be playing with a cleek that had a shaft slightly bent over. I observed that in putting with this cleek the balls seemed to run with more accuracy than usual, and, following up the idea, the patent putter was produced. It is difficult to explain the principle of this club. With an ordinary putter the stroke is of the nature of a push, while with this patent it is more a pull than a push. It has also the advantage of allowing the player to see the blade of the cleek while addressing the ball, as the line of the shaft is in front of the blade. Although I run the risk of being accused of partiality for my own patents, I cannot refrain from saying that I find I can putt much better with this club than with any other I have hitherto tried, and I have received testimonials in its favour from many of the best players of the day, both amateur and professional.

The Driving-putter is really a driver with a short, stiff shaft and a deep face, more upright than an ordinary driver and flatter than an ordinary putter, and it is used for playing long putts and also for driving against a head wind; the shortness and stiffness of the shaft ensure accuracy, and less tendency to pull or heel the ball.

Driving-irons have less loft than usual, and are used for strokes shorter in distance than a cleek shot, and yet beyond the reach of an ordinary iron.

Lofting-irons have more loft, as their name implies, and are used for wrist shots and short approaches, lofts over hazards and similar strokes. The chief object of these irons is to pitch the ball on to the green in such a way as to make it run as short a distance as possible after alighting. It must be borne in mind that the more loft there is on an iron the more difficult is the club to handle, and any errors in judgment or in striking the ball are the more severely punished. The reason for this is explained hereafter in the chapter relating to approaching.

Having given a general explanation of the various clubs most frequently used, I will now endeavour to give some directions for the guidance of the player in selecting a suitable set

from the stock which will be open to him for inspection when he makes his choice.

The materials principally used in the construction of clubs are: for the heads of wooden clubs, beech and apple; for the heads of metal clubs, malleable iron and gun-metal; and for shafts, hickory white and brown, ash, lancewood, orange-wood, bloomahoo, greenheart, purpleheart, and lemonwood. It must not be supposed that the above is by any means an exhaustive catalogue, because as a matter of fact many other varieties of wood have been tried, and are daily being tried.

Wooden clubs are most extensively made with beech heads and hickory shafts. Apple heads are also made, but the supply of that wood is so limited that it can scarcely be got, and it does not make such a good driving club as beech.

Beginners, especially those who are hard hitters, until they get into the proper way of striking the ball, find it difficult to get a club that will last them any length of time. An ordinary club-head will not resist the strain of a hard topped ball, or a ball hit off the neck; and besides the annoyance and vexation, not to speak of the expense of such breakages, players frequently find great difficulty in getting a club exactly the same as the broken one. Clubs are like individuals – no two are alike, however similar in appearance they may be – and if you break your favourite club, you have, so to speak, to serve an apprenticeship to another before you can use it as well as its predecessor. Complaints about the frailty of all wooden clubs having been frequently made to me, I endeavoured to manufacture a club-head which, while able to stand more strain than a beech head, would yet not be inferior in driving power, and for some time past I have been making club-heads of wood compressed and otherwise treated to make it more enduring. In this club the wood forming the head is bent so that the grain runs down the neck and along the head, making it practically unbreakable; and, in fact, I guarantee that with ordinary tear and wear such heads are indestructible.

Many players like their clubs to have leather faces, and I am rather in favour of this. Leather faces were originally devised for repairing clubs that had become damaged by tear and wear, but they are now frequently put into quite new heads. A leather face put into a new club helps to make it last better, and when put into a damaged club will often save the head from breaking, and permit of its being used for a considerable time longer. This in a favourite club is no small matter, and whenever signs of tear and wear begin to show, it is as well to get the repair made at once.

Good club-shafts are considerably more difficult to get than good heads. The words 'good shaft' have a world of meaning. Here are some of the requisites. The wood must be light in actual weight; the grain must run straight down the stick; it must be supple and yet not wobbly, and have a fine steely spring, without being too stiff, throughout all its length, gently tapered from the leather grip to the scare. Any one who has examined a lot of shafts will know the difficulty of obtaining a piece of wood with even several of these requisites.

Hickory, either white or brown, makes the best shaft. The other woods mentioned I consider to be too heavy for good shafts for driving-clubs – using these words in the generic term to include brassies and spoons. Even in hickory there are great differences in the weight of the wood. Ash makes a good shaft, but is as a rule too supple for anything but a light head. Greenheart is too heavy for any clubs except iron niblicks and putters. Lemonwood makes a good shaft, but is rather heavy; it does very well, however, for shafting iron clubs, and it has a fine steely spring and keeps its straightness, being less liable to warp than hickory.

A set of golf-clubs consists of from six to ten clubs for ordinary players. The six most useful clubs are – driver, brassy, cleek, iron, and putter, and a mashie or a niblick, depending on the green to which the player belongs. If his green be a seaside one, where the chief hazards are sand bunkers, then I recommend a niblick as the best club for taking the ball out of such hazards; while, on the other hand, if his green be an inland one, where there are not usually many such hazards, then I recommend a mashie as more useful for pitching the ball over walls and cops, and extricating it from heavy lies in long grass, and as also useful for playing approaches. The other clubs mentioned before may be added to the set as the player finds occasion for their use, and as his style of play demands. He will not be long in finding out the clubs he plays best with.

Face to face with the clubs he has to select from, the first difficulty to a beginner will probably be, 'What should be the length of my club?' The usual length of a driver from the top of the shaft right down to the sole at the heel is about forty-four or forty-five inches, and an inch or two more or less will be found to suit most players. It is not possible to lay down any arbitrary rule whereby a player may be guided in choosing his club. The length of the shaft depends upon the player. It is a fallacy to suppose that it is in every case regulated by stature. No doubt this has a good deal to do with the matter; but tall men sometimes play with very short clubs, while, on the other hand, players under average height sometimes use very long clubs. It depends chiefly upon the relation of the player's stance to his ball. If he stands near the ball his club will be more upright – that is to say, the angle of the shaft and head will be less, and hence the shaft will be shorter; while if he stands back from the ball, the club will be flatter, and the shaft consequently longer. It depends, too, upon the hold or grip he takes of his club – whether he grips the extreme end of the shaft or places his hands lower down. Most command can usually be obtained over a short upright club, and consequently the hitting is more accurate. For that reason, and for the reasons after explained in the chapter on style, I am inclined to recommend clubs that do not lie too flat. On a comparison of the clubs of to-day with those made long ago, it would appear that they have become much shorter in the shaft.

The weight of the head is another matter that depends entirely upon the player. Some play with a heavy club, while others using a light club drive every bit as far, and play just as well. The distance a ball is driven depends upon the swiftness of the stroke, and not upon the heaviness of it, and each player will in time find out by experience the weight of club with which he can deal the ball the swiftest blow – that is the proper weight for him. A light club is best in the hands of most players: with a heavy club a golfer is apt to get into a bad loose style of play, or, to use the golfing phrase, 'it swings him off his feet.' This applies specially to those who have a full swing. With a half swing a heavier club may be used with more effect than a light one; but, as will be explained hereafter, a half swing is not a good golfing style, and is not to be encouraged.

The most important feature in all clubs is what is technically known as the 'balance' or 'feel.' It is hardly possible to describe accurately in word what this mystic quality consists of. The weight of the head, the weight of the shaft, and its stiffness or suppleness, and the thickness of the grip, each and all play an important part in determining the balance of a club. It may be stated, however, that a well-balanced club should have a sweet, easy feel when handled and swung, and it should neither feel as if there was a dead weight at the head, nor as if there was no weight at all – all the parts must be proportioned one to the other. An experienced player has no difficulty in at once deciding whether a club be well balanced or not, and unless a golfer has sufficient knowledge to judge for himself, he had better trust to the judgment and advice of some reliable person, either a golfing friend or the maker from whom he purchases.

The would-be golfer having an eye to the fitness of things will probably begin by selecting a driver – the club with which he takes the first stroke at the tee. Having the maker's stock before him, some drivers will no doubt be placed in his hands for approval. Let him take one, and, standing upright, grasp the handle with both hands – having previously made up his mind as to the proper part of the handle to be grasped – and lay the head flat on the ground as if in the act of playing. If he feels that the club fits him comfortably, it will be about the proper length for him. The head is the better of having a good breadth of wood across the top, and a good depth of face, but should be well proportioned in every part, and not clumsy. The lead and bone should be carefully fitted into their respective places, and shaft and head neatly bound together. I have advised the selection of a club having a good breadth of wood across the head, and such a club will suit the majority of golfers. The shaft should be perfectly straight and the tapering very gradual. If too sudden the result is either that the spring will be entirely confined to a small portion just above the scare, in which case the shaft will be deficient in driving power, as the upper part will be nearly rigid, or that while there may be some spring in the upper part, it will be so stiff as to require considerable exertion to bring it out and make it available for driving the ball; consequently the club will require to be grasped very firmly, entailing unnecessary fatigue to the player. There should be just a sufficient amount of suppleness in the shaft to give life to the club. If there be too much the club is sure to have a wobbly feel. The spring or suppleness should lie in the whole shaft, from the scare to right up under the leather, but should be most perceptible in the lower part. The grip (*i.e.* the leather handle which is grasped) of the club should not be too thick, neither should it be too thin, but of the two it is better to be on the thin side. It will be observed that, when a club-head is laid flat upon the ground beside the ball, the face of one will lie in to the ball, while another will lie off, and a third will be quite straight. They are all equally good, and individual players can please themselves in their choice.

The above remarks hold good as regards choosing all wooden driving clubs. In brassies and spoons the shaft should be somewhat stiffer than in the driver, and of course there must be more loft on the faces. With regard to brassies, I would point out that some makers, considering the brass sole sufficient protection to the club-head, omit the usual 'bone' with which all wooden clubs should be protected at the bottom of the face; but players should not accept such clubs. Without the bone the wooden face gets hammered in by repeated strokes, and the result is that the brass sole, being left projecting, cuts the ball, not to say the turf of the links. See therefore that the brassy has a bone in it. Brassy-niblicks, it has been stated, are smaller in the heads than other wooden clubs. There is a limit to this, however, and it is a mistake to get one with too small a head. It is essential that the face should be deep.

All wooden clubs should be squarely made at the neck, as this brings the head into a more direct line with the shaft, and seems to give the club more power. I do not say they should be made square, but a long, rounded neck should be avoided, as it not only carries the head further out of the line of the shaft, but weakens the strength and durability of the head. I have heard such clubs called 'juke-neckit' (*i.e.* duck necked), and the term describes, not inaptly, their appearance.

Brassies and long-spoons should be rather flatter in the lie than a driver. The latter club is most in use for tee-shots, and even if it lies slightly on the heel – and indeed some players prefer their drivers to lie on the heel and not flat on the sole when addressing the ball – this does not prevent the ball from being perfectly and truly struck owing to its being raised up on the tee. But brassies and spoons are more frequently used through the green, where the ball lies close to the surface of the ground, and in that case it is essential that the sole of the club should be flat on the ground to enable the ball to be picked up clean. A club lying on its heel would, in playing through the green, be apt to get away a half-topped ball, and it need hardly be said that this would interfere with the distance of the stroke.

With regard to metal clubs, it is best to obtain those made of iron – gun-metal is too soft to withstand the hard usage they have to undergo, and heads of the latter metal consequently soon get damaged and useless. For putters gun-metal is not so objectionable; but even for them iron is better, as they are frequently used for running up long strokes on a hard level green with short turf. The heads, of whatever they are made, should be free from flaws in the metal, and should be sharply and squarely made; that is to say, the socket and blade should be rather angled than rounded off.

In selecting a cleek, the following are some of the points to be observed. The blade should not be too long – rather short, in fact – and it should neither be too deep nor too narrow, and of a fair thickness. The tendency of the present day is to make the blade much shorter and considerably thicker than the older makers did, and I must say I favour the innovation. For an ordinary cleek for all-round play, the blade is the better of being rather thicker at the bottom than at the top, as this helps to make the ball rise. The thicker the blade is at the bottom, and the thinner at the top, the more does the cleek tend to loft the ball, apart altogether from actual pitch on the face. Hence cleeks are made with less gradation of thickness in metal than are irons. All the same, there should be some gradation; and it is well, too, to get a cleek with loft, as being more capable of general use. With a driving-cleek it is of course different, but the peculiarities of driving-cleeks have already been referred to. The socket of the cleek, *i.e.* the part into which the shaft is fitted, should be short and light, so as to enable more weight to be put into the blade. The shaft of a cleek should be comparatively stiff.

The above remarks apply also to selecting an iron or a mashie. In playing with an iron it is usual, for the reason explained in Chapter v, to take away a little turf with the stroke, and consequently the blade is made deeper than in the cleek. With the view of assisting to loft the ball, it is also made much thicker at the bottom of the blade than at the top, and it should have a good deal more loft than the cleek. The iron should be a tolerably heavy club, heavier than the cleek. As before pointed out, it is usual to take turf in iron play, and unless the club used be a fairly heavy one, there will be loss of force. A heavy iron will cut its way through when a light one will stick in the ground. These remarks apply to irons for all-round use, because in the case of a lofting-iron it is of advantage to have a slightly lighter club, as enabling a more delicate stroke to be played. The shaft of an iron should be perfectly stiff. By this I do not mean rigid and not flexible; there must, of course, be spring in it, but it should be so stiff as to require some force to bring out the spring. An iron with a wobbly shaft is useless. Great accuracy in hitting the ball is required for all iron strokes, and it is not possible to obtain this when the player has not complete control over the head of his club, which he cannot have when it is at the end of a wobbly stick.

The mashie should have more loft than either cleek or iron, and for all-round work should be as heavy as the iron. It should be made square at the nose, and have a deep face tapered from the bottom to the top, and, like an iron, should have a stiff shaft.

The niblick, most of all clubs, requires weight, because it is intended for the rough work of extricating the ball from bunkers and hazards, and it is of great advantage to get force into the stroke. The head is all the better of being tolerably large, but an experienced player may use one with a smaller head. It is possibly unnecessary to say that there must be a good deal of loft on the face. The shaft of the club should be strong and stiff, and not too long.

Next and last come putters. How much could be written on this subject! and where is the golfer who has not got his own peculiar opinion about putting? If a golf-club has ever brought a fancy price, inquiry will almost invariably elicit the fact that that club was a wooden putter. The most essential requisites for a putter are that it be perfectly true in the face, and that the balance be good. Of all wooden clubs it should be the longest in the head, but there is no great necessity for breadth of wood, nor for depth of face, as in other wooden clubs, provided that it be shapely. It is an advantage to have a club that lies well, and in this case the face should lie slightly in to the ball. The head should have a good deal of weight more than any other wooden club. Some players prefer the shaft to have a slight curve, the concavity being towards the player; but this is more a matter of taste than anything else. A straight shaft is quite as good, so long as it is not bent down – that is to say, so long as the concavity is not from the player. There is generally no loft, or at most just a sensation, on the face of a wooden putter. Iron putters are very numerous; all that need be said is to repeat what is before stated, that put-

ting-cleeks are to be preferred with the faces very slightly lofted to prevent the ball from springing. A properly hit ball lying
on a smooth putting-green will not spring; it is only when it
happens to lie in a nick that this danger arises, and then it is
more liable to spring off a wooden putter than off a cleek. The
narrow sole of a cleek enables it to fit closer in to the ball, and
so pick it out, while the broad sole of a wooden putter prevents its doing so. The shafts of all putters should be quite stiff
and short, so as to give power and command over the club.

It may be taken as a general rule that there should be a
gradation in the length of the different clubs in the following
order, viz.: driver, brassy, cleek, iron, mashie or niblick, and
putter – the driver being the longest, the putter the shortest,
and the others ranging between these two extremes. In adding
other clubs to the set, the same order will be observed – driving-clubs being longer, clubs for approaching shorter, and putters shortest of all. In the same way there will be a gradation
in the loft upon the face: drivers will have little or no loft,
while brassies and spoons will be set back or lofted. Cleeks
among iron clubs will have least loft, and irons a little or a
good deal more, depending upon the purpose for which they
are to be used – for driving or for pitching. Putters, as has been
mentioned, should have very little loft, if any. I would recommend that, in the first instance, serviceable all-round clubs be
obtained – for example, an ordinary cleek and a medium-
pitched iron. It is much better for a player to get at first one
iron with a medium amount of pitch, than to get both a driving-iron and a lofting-iron. After experience is obtained and
proficiency acquired, other clubs can be added to the set.

To an absolute novice I would give this counsel, 'Learn the
game with the clubs you intend to play with hereafter.' So far
as I know, there are not special clubs made for beginners. Such
advice must of course be used with discretion, and adapted to
the peculiar circumstances of each case. For example, a hard
hitter should see that he purchases strong clubs that will stand
some bad usage, because he cannot at first always expect to
get the ball off the centre of the face. Most clubs will stand a

fair amount of tear and wear, but in the hands of a powerful hitter the life of a wooden head is bound to be shorter, unless counterbalanced by stronger make. Difficulty may be experienced in getting the ball up with a driver, in which case the use of a spooned club in the initial stages of tuition may be beneficial. Under no circumstances is it expedient to begin by using only a cleek or other iron club. A great many faulty styles of golf can be traced to such a practice.

While a good game can be played with comparatively few clubs, the addition of two or three more to a set will frequently obviate the necessity of having to play difficult strokes. So long as a full stroke has to be played there is no great risk of making any mistake; it is when three-quarter and half shots are necessary that the greatest risk of foozling exists. Half shots it is not possible to avoid; but by judiciously selecting a few extra clubs with varying degrees of loft on them, three-quarter shots may be almost entirely evaded, and the number of long half shots requiring to be played considerably reduced, full strokes with one or other of the extra clubs coming in their place.

Lofting-irons and lofting-mashies are before noticed. I recommend the former in preference to the latter. The blade of the iron is larger than the blade of the mashie, and there is thus a larger surface available for hitting the ball when the former is used. Mashies require very accurate play, especially for lofting strokes. Although the niblick is the best club for bunker play, a heavy mashie is very serviceable for this purpose; and it is quite possible to get a mashie that will not only answer for playing approaches, but also for the rougher work of digging the ball out of hazards. The bunkers are, however, apt to spoil the mashie for the more delicate work of approaching.

For putting, the appropriate club is undoubtedly a putter, wooden or metal; but all the same some very fine players have putted, and putted magnificently, with an ordinary cleek. On a rough green a cleek does well, because by playing the ball with 'bottom' or back spin on it, it is less liable to be deflected by irregularities of the green. Nothing, however, can beat a putting cleek for all-round play.

All the clubs above mentioned are made to suit left-handed players. It is a mistake to suppose that a man otherwise left-handed should play golf with left-handed clubs. The proportion of left-handed golfers is almost infinitesimal, and they are all amateurs. I do not know of a single left-handed professional player. There is no reason, however, why left-handed players should not excel at golf, and, as a matter of fact, I know several who would be hard to beat. Nevertheless, I think beginners should follow the usual style of play; and although in a matter of this kind every one must please himself, I would urge all who are for the first time taking up golf to play with right-handed clubs, notwithstanding that they may be naturally left-handed. It has been recommended by some authorities on the game that a left-handed club should be included in every player's set, to meet the case of a ball lying up against a wall, or in some such position where it cannot be easily struck with a right-handed club. Such a plan is no doubt good; but unless he has had some previous practice, it is not an easy matter for a man who uses right-handed clubs to pick up a left-handed club and play a stroke, particularly a difficult one, with it. He will probably miss the ball altogether if he attempts to do any such thing.

The greatest secret, if secret it be, of playing well with any club is to know it thoroughly – to know what strokes it can best be used for, and when to use it, and to have confidence, which can only be gained by past successes, in being able to do what is required.

Balance in a club has been spoken of. This quality is so subtle that the least alteration may spoil it for ever. Be very careful, therefore, not to tamper with a well-balanced club. The mere putting of a new leather on the handle may spoil the balance, and it is better to have a well-balanced club with a tattered and patched-up leather, than to have a badly balanced one with a perfectly new leather.

The keeping of clubs in order is a matter to which a good share of attention has been directed, and it is frequently recommended that the shaft and head should be kept slightly oiled. If the clubs are properly cared for, and not kept in either too damp or too dry a place, I do not advise oiling, as I find it is apt to cause cracks in the wood. Before a club leaves the maker's hands it receives a coating of oil and varnish, and this ought to be sufficient to last for a long time. If, however, the clubs have been allowed to get dry, a touch of oil will render them less brittle; but care must be taken that the oil is not too liberally applied, and it should not be allowed to come into contact with the scare, the face, the sole, or other unvarnished parts of the head. A very slight touch is sufficient, and after application the club should be well rubbed up and polished with a dry cloth. If the coating of varnish has worn off, it should be renewed, as a protection against wet getting into the wood. A really fine club should not be used on a wet day, if it can be avoided, as not only will the head probably be ruined, but also the shaft. I have seen some splendid shafts, with just the right spring in them, rendered wobbly and absolutely useless through their getting thoroughly soaked by playing in wet weather.

Iron clubs are usually polished round, not down, the socket and along the blade. After polishing the face of the blade lengthwise, the heel and toe thereof are rubbed across. The different rubbings are easily visible, and cause a distinctive mark of about a couple of inches in the centre of the face, which acts as a guide to the eye in playing. Irons should be polished with very fine emery cloth, and not too much rubbed. Each polishing helps to rub away the metal, and in course of time diminishes the weight of the head. A drop of oil on the back of the cloth will prevent the emery from coming off in small pieces, as it is somewhat apt to do.

Golf Balls, etc.

Without going into history, it may briefly be stated that in the early part of the century the only golf-ball in use was the old feather ball, which was made by forcing feathers into a

spherical leathern case. The introduction of gutta-percha rev-
olutionised ball-making, and gutta-percha balls have now
entirely superseded the feather balls, which are only to be seen
among relics of the past. Gutta-percha balls were, speaking of
modern times, in the first place moulded round, and then
notched by being hand-hammered with a hammer for the purpose. Experience has proved that unless balls are notched they
will not fly. After notching they were painted white or red as
occasion required, and were then ready for the market. Hand-
hammered balls have within the last dozen years been superseded by machine-made balls, which go through the same
processes, except that the notching is done by machinery
instead of the hand, and these in turn are being superseded by
balls which are moulded and notched at one and the same
time. Different makers have generally distinctive arrangements
of the notches on the balls to distinguish more readily their
makes; but it need scarcely be said that although the notching
is of the utmost importance, one arrangement is as good as
another.

It may be explained that the balls painted white are those
most usually seen and played with, those painted red being
used for playing when the ground is covered with snow – for
in Scotland a slight snowfall does not prevent the more ardent
golfers from indulging in their favourite game.

Golf-balls are made in the following sizes, viz. 26, 27,
27½, 28, and 29, these figures representing the weight in
drachms avoirdupois; 26's and 29's, the two extremes, are not
much used, the one being considered too light and the other
too heavy.

Gutta-percha is not without a rival: balls are made of various compositions, of which gutta-percha is a component part,
and rival authorities uphold the merits of their favourite ball
with no little vehemence. The controversy waged on this subject has caused the balls to be known as the 'gutty' and the
'putty' respectively. These are for all practical purposes the
only two kinds of ball in the market. Celluloid has been tried,
but up to the present time has not proved to be a formidable

competitor against the others.

Of the gutty and the putty balls the former are the harder in substance, and there is no mistaking the sharp, firm click emitted when struck. The putty has quite a different feel to the player, as it is heavier for its size and is softer – it has more of an indiarubbery nature, in fact. A putty ball does not carry so far as a gutty, but at the end of its flight it has considerably more running power. Its adherents maintain that it is less liable to be deflected by side winds, and that it will glide over or run through hazards in which a gutty would stick, and it cannot be denied that it possesses the last-mentioned quality. Notwithstanding this, I consider the advantages of the gutty ball more than make up for any disadvantages. It is always an object in playing the long game to get a ball that will carry as far as possible, and here the superiority of the gutta-percha ball is undoubted. The player who uses a putty ball will also find that it will not rise so quickly off the club as its rival; and hence, if the ball be lying in a hollow, or close to a rising face, he may have to play the stroke with an iron, whereas, using a gutty ball, he might be able to take a brassy or a cleek. In approaching, the running power which a putty ball possesses renders it difficult to make it fall dead, and all golfers know how great an advantage it is to be able to do this. For putting, too, the gutties are more manageable than the putties, which roll about the green and are apt to run over the hole instead of going in. For these reasons I recommend gutta-percha balls.

The sort of ball he uses is not, to a beginner, a matter of much importance, but it is better that he should, from the first, use that to which he intends to adhere.

In selecting gutty balls, care should be taken to see that they are at least six months old; but they should not be much older than this, as, if so, the paint is apt to chip off, and they lose some of their elasticity. They should be good 'stotters' – that is to say, when dropped on a flagstone or pavement they should rebound with a clear, hard click, and those that rebound furthest are generally the best. Some balls when placed in water will float, while others will sink. I prefer those that sink, because they are heavier than the others. Floaters are too light; they leave the club quickly, and their carry is soon exhausted. The size of ball most generally used is 27½, but the larger it is the better, as, in putting, a big ball will fall into the hole more readily than a small one, and is less likely, from its weight, to be deflected by a stiff blade of grass or such obstacle on the green. Of course it requires more strength to play with a big heavy ball than with a light one, and I would say to golfers, 'Play with as big a ball as you are able to manage comfortably.' A golfer who is not a hard hitter will probably play best with a ball that floats in water, but a strong player will knock such a ball out of shape in a very few strokes. Experience will teach every one the ball best adapted to his game better than anything that can be written on the subject. Some makers have recently brought out balls made of selected material, which are sold at a correspondingly selected price. I think, however, that they are too light in weight, and for a powerful player ordinary balls are preferable.

After a ball has been played with a few times the life gets knocked out of it, and it loses the elasticity which characterises a new ball. Although not good enough for using in an important match, it is good enough for practice; but by degrees it will become useless, from hacks made with clubs and the chipping off of the paint. Balls arrived at this stage can be remade at moderate cost; but in remaking there is always a slight loss of material, and thus a 27½ when remade will be scarcely larger than a 27. Remade balls are not as a rule so good as new balls; at the same time, a ball remade for the first time is not much inferior, and I could name certain balls that are rather improved by the remaking process. After being remade a couple of times any ball is useless, as it gets too small, and fresh gutta-percha cannot be added satisfactorily.

A few years ago golf-clubs were carried in a loose bundle and secured by a strap round the shafts when not in use, but nowadays most golfers carry them in a bag for the purpose. Such a bag is a useful requisite, and in wet weather it helps to keep the clubs dry. 'Caddie bags,' as they are called, are made in different styles to suit individual tastes. They are practically all equally good so long as they are sufficient for the protection of the clubs.

It is absolutely essential that a golfer's shoulders should be free for the swing of the club; and he must therefore take care to see that his coat, and indeed his whole clothing, is so loose as not to interfere with perfect freedom of motion. It used to be the almost invariable rule for golfers to wear red coats. After being to some extent discarded, red coats are again coming into fashion, and I think that the good old custom should be adhered to. Each club usually adopts for its uniform a red coat with distinctive collar, facings, or buttons, and the members of the various clubs should be enjoined to wear their club-coats. More important than his coat are a golfer's boots or shoes. It is not possible to play golf unless a firm stance is obtained, and therefore the soles of the boots or shoes should be studded with nails or 'tackets.' It is better to have the tackets put in singly, an inch or so apart, over the sole, than in groups of three or four; the latter do not give such a firm hold, more particularly after a little wear. It is with the fore part of the sole and the toe that the hold is taken, and when any nails come out they should be replaced. Rubber soled boots and shoes are good in their way, and in dry weather take a better hold of hard, slippery ground, but for all-round wear they are not equal to tackety-boots.

Golfers with tender hands frequently find it necessary to wear gloves. If the hands will not harden naturally, I do not know of any effectual remedy except gloves. The play of gentlemen who wear them does not seem to be prejudicially affected thereby. This is, however, a subject on which I cannot speak from personal experience, as I have never tried the experiment of wearing gloves.

CHAPTER THREE

Style of Play

IT IS OF THE FIRST importance that a golfer should have a good style of play, these words being here used as including grip of club, stance, and swing. One frequently hears it said, 'What does my style signify provided I can play a good game?' To this I would reply, 'In the majority of cases it is hardly possible to play a good game unless you have a good style.' It is also said

FIG. 4 – THE GRIP – FIRST STAGE

that if the best golfers be closely watched no two of them have the same style, and which among all these styles is the correct one? My answer to this is that there are few crack players who have not a good style, and that although there may be, and

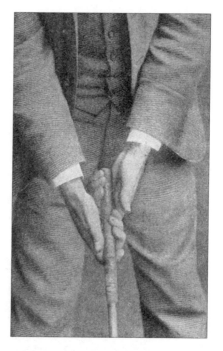

FIG. 5 – THE GRIP – SECOND STAGE

undoubtedly are, many whose styles are different in detail, they are fundamentally the same – they are all modelled on the recognised lines. There are, however, among the followers of every game men whose play can hardly be excelled, and who yet violate the canons of style. Such players have been termed geniuses, and a few are to be found among the ranks of golfers; but I would further say that these are the exceptions that prove the rule. The imitators of geniuses seldom attain to

FIG. 6 – THE GRIP – COMPLETE

any perfection, and generally find it difficult to reach mediocrity. For geniuses no rules can be laid down – their success justifies their play, but only their success. Failure would heap on their heads deserved ridicule.

I would recommend all golfers to model their styles upon the recognised lines that have stood the test of decades of play at the hands of the best amateurs and professionals. If any one finds himself to be a genius, he can easily carve out his own

FIG. 7 – A GRIP NOT RECOMMENDED

peculiar style, and will be none the worse, but probably much the better, for having begun upon the orthodox lines.

The first detail is the grip of the club, and it is a matter of considerable importance, as upon it depends to some extent the swing. Very many players who study the swing entirely neglect to see that their hands are in the right position, and consequently their styles can never be good. With the view of showing the proper grip, I propose to describe it somewhat

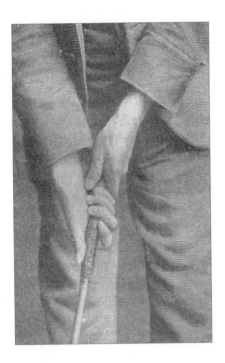

FIG. 8 – A GRIP NOT RECOMMENDED

minutely. The illustrations will show that it is really the grasp any one would naturally take. Let the club be placed horizontally, the handle being towards the player; then let him place his hands alongside of it, as shown in Fig. 4. All he has then to do is to close his fingers round the handle without moving his arms, and he has the correct grip. The handle should not lie across the palms of the hands, but across the roots of the fingers, and it is the fingers that should hold the club. Fig. 5

FIG. 9 – THE GRIP – POSITION OF HANDS AT TOP OF SWING

shows the second stage, viz. the club held in the ringers, and Fig. 6 shows the complete grip. The thumbs should neither be wound round the shaft, as shown in Fig. 7, nor should they lie along it, as shown in Fig. 8, but should cross it obliquely, and touch the point of the fingers, as already illustrated in Fig. 6. Of the grips shown in Figs. 7 and 8, the last is by far the more objectionable of the two, because the position of the thumbs in that case prevents the club being properly swung round the

FIG. 10 – THE GRIP – POSITION OF HANDS AT TOP OF SWING
(BACK VIEW)

shoulders. At the same time I must state, in fairness to a number of first-class players, that although this grip (Fig. 8) is never adopted by any of them for driving, it is sometimes used in playing half shots and in putting. The grip shown in Fig. 7

45

is frequently adopted by cricketers who take up golfing; but I consider that in the majority of cases it does not give the player such a complete command over his club as the grip shown in Fig. 6. Although I do not advocate its adoption, it is, how-

FIG. 11 – THE GRIP – A BAD POSITION OF HANDS AT TOP OF SWING

ever, a grip that I cannot absolutely condemn; but for approaching and putting it is less delicate than the recognised grip. With regard to what I have just stated as to players using different grips for driving and for the short game, I hardly think it is advisable to follow that practice. Golfers must please themselves; but the opinion I hold, and which I follow out in practice, is to simplify the game as much as possible; and if one style of grip is sufficient and equally good for all parts of the game, why have two? I therefore unhesitatingly recommend the recognised grip (Fig. 6) as that most suitable for driving, approaching, and putting. The hands should be close together, touching each other. There should not be a space between them. As a general rule it may be laid down that the fingers of both hands should grasp the club firmly, but those of the left should have the firmer hold: the theory is that the left hand holds the club while the right guides it. This rule is, however, subject to certain exceptions, as will hereafter be pointed out. The club should not be held too tightly, as this wearies the hands and wrists without any benefit being derived therefrom. If it be held sufficiently firmly to prevent its slipping or turning, this is all that is required; holding any tighter is a mistake, and a useless expenditure of force.

It must not be supposed that when once the club is grasped the hands are to remain fixed and rigid in the position taken up. As the club is swung back the arms go with it, necessitating the wrists being flexed, and the hands must open until at the top of the swing they assume the position shown in Figs. 9 and 10, which respectively show from the front and back view the hands at the top of the swing. But although the hands are opened up, the grasp of the fingers is still maintained. In teaching beginners, more especially ladies, I have found that there is a strong tendency to endeavour to keep the hands immovable, which results in a position something like that shown in Fig. 11. Such a position, apart altogether from being stiff and uncomfortable, is fatal to a good swing.

Different players grasp different parts of the handle of the club. Some grip the club so far down the shaft that the right hand is below the leather. Others go to the opposite extreme and grasp the very end of the shaft, and others different parts of the intervening space. The exact part of the handle grasped is not an essential point. It will frequently be found that the difference depends in some degree upon the weight of the club used. Golfers who play with light clubs will almost invariably be found to grasp the end of the shaft, while those who use heavy clubs will grasp lower down. The grip low down on the shaft is not, however, to be recommended, because it shortens the circle traversed by the club head, and hence detracts from driving power. For myself, I may say I grasp the extreme end of the club – my left hand actually covers the end of the shaft; in fact, I lay it in the palm of that hand, the right hand being immediately below. Now, my reason for this is that from experience I find this grip gives the left hand sufficient power to prevent the club slipping, and lessens the tendency, which naturally exists, of endeavouring to guide the club with it, which frequently results in pulling and slicing. There is an innate tendency to guide with both hands, and the influence exerted by the left hand is generally such that it twists the club in its descent, thereby causing pulling or slicing, and I find that by grasping the extreme end of the shaft with the left hand its power to twist the club is thereby lessened. It is above stated that I lay the end of the club in the palm of my left hand; strictly speaking, this is not quite an accurate expression, because, as before pointed out, the club shaft should be placed at the root of the fingers.

The position of the ball and the stance are the next matters for consideration. Great diversity of practice exists in regard to the distance players stand from the ball, some standing quite near it, and others preferring that it should be just within reach. I do not believe in either extreme. If the ball is too far away from the player the whole position is apt to be stiff, and if too near it is apt to be cramped. The ball should neither be too near the player nor too far away – just within easy reach. To lay down a measurement is impossible, because the position depends upon the stature of the player, the length and lie of his club, and the length of his arms. The most particular direction that can be given is to grasp the club according to the instructions before given, lay the head down flat beside the ball, the arms being held easy, slightly bent at the

FIG. 12 — THE DRIVE — ADDRESSING THE BALL — SIDE VIEW

FIG. 13 — THE DRIVE — ADDRESSING THE BALL — FRONT VIEW

elbows, and in towards the body rather than out from it as shown in Fig. 12, and take up the stance at such a distance from the ball as will enable it to be struck comfortably and easily in the course of the swing without either bending for-

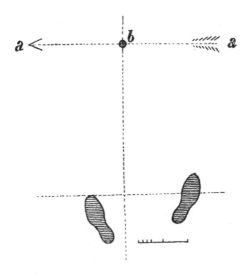

FIG. 14 – THE DRIVE – DIAGRAM OF POSITION

ward to reach it or cramping the swing by standing too near. The club being laid beside the ball, and the player standing as far back as he conveniently is able, will form a general index of the proper distance between the player and the ball.

With regard to the stance, the ball should be opposite the player's body, and the feet so far apart as to ensure a firm hold of the ground without straddling the legs and without turning out the toes too much. These are the most particular directions I can undertake to give. To make the position more intelligible there are given illustrations (Fig. 12 side view, and Fig. 13

front view) of the writer in the position for driving, or, as it is technically termed, 'addressing the ball' for a drive, and a diagram, or what may be called a ground-plan (Fig. 14). In the diagram (which is drawn to a scale) the line of play is indicated by *aa*, and *b* is the ball.

The relative distances between the feet, and between the feet and the ball, cannot be laid down by actual measurement to suit every one; but the scale will enable the curious to make exact measurements of my stance, although, I am afraid, they will not profit very much therefrom. The illustrations and diagram will convey a better idea of the positions than can be obtained from pages of description, and all I propose to add is that the position should be easy.

A comparison of what has been written with Figs. 12, 13, and 14 will probably draw forth the remark that my own stance only complies very generally with the directions given, and this I am quite willing to admit. I say it is not possible to lay down hard and fast lines – all that can be done is to give a very rough outline of the fundamental position. It will be observed that I place the ball nearly opposite the heel of my left foot – about a couple of inches more to the right – and that the right foot is slightly advanced. That is my own particular style; but it is far from my intention to dogmatise and say that, because I adopt it, it is the only right one, and that all others are wrong. The ball may be moved to the right or left of the place shown in the diagram, and the feet may be placed in the same line, or either the right or the left foot may be advanced. These are merely variations of a fundamental principle, and do not mark a defective or bad style unless exaggerated. This much I may say, however, that it may be taken as a general rule, that if the feet are placed in the same parallel line, it will be found that the ball should be teed almost exactly opposite the left heel; if the right foot is drawn back the ball will be placed slightly further to the left, and if the right foot is advanced the ball will be placed somewhat more to the right. This rule, I need hardly point out, must be applied with discretion. It is possible to draw back or to advance the right foot to

FIG. 15 – THE DRIVE – MR LAIDLAY ADDRESSING THE BALL

such an extent as to make a comfortable stance an impossibility, and in the same way it is possible to move the position of the ball to the left or right of the line of the player's left heel so much as to render accurate hitting of the ball extremely unlikely. A few inches to one side or other of the position indicated in the diagram may be regarded as covering the limits of any desirable alteration. The exact position of the ball opposite the player depends upon his stance, as, if the right foot be drawn back and the ball placed much to the right of the left heel, there is great danger of the club face hanging over the ball and foundering it; and, on the other hand, if the right foot is advanced and the ball placed to the left, there is an equal danger of the ball being hooked. The older writers on the subject recommend the placing of the ball opposite the player's left heel, and the feet in a parallel line; but, to my knowledge, many of the finest players of bygone days stood with the right foot in advance, and teed the ball to the right of the position indicated by these writers. This mode of standing with the right foot in advance is becoming more and more popular, and the majority of our best players adopt that stance. My experience of the different positions leads me to the strong belief that the best stance is that with the right foot slightly advanced and the ball placed a little to the right of a line drawn out from the left heel, and for these reasons: The other position (which corresponds to 'off the left leg' in approach play) develops a wild style of golf, and a strong tendency to pull the ball, because it discourages a proper follow-through. Owing to the right foot being so far back, the player cannot at the end of the swing front the direction in which he desires to drive, and the body pivots on the left foot, thereby encouraging the club to swing *round the body*. On the other hand, the position which is recommended – viz. that off the right leg – leaves the player at the end of the swing fronting the direction of the drive, and in as nearly as possible the position any one would take up who intended to walk after his ball in the line of flight, thus enabling the arms to be well thrown out after the ball, and encouraging a follow-through. The object of the follow-through is hereafter explained. While expressing these views in regard to driving off the left leg, I feel bound to state that Mr J E Laidlay adopts that position; in fact, I believe that, were it not for his play, there would be fewer references to this particular style. Than Mr Laidlay there is not a steadier or a better golfer, as is amply proved by his achievements during the past number of years. Mr Laidlay has somewhat altered his stance

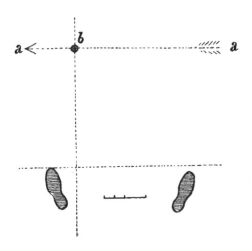

FIG. 16 – THE DRIVE – DIAGRAM OF MR LAIDLAY'S POSITION

within the last year or two, but it is still 'off the left leg.' An illustration (Fig. 15) and a diagram (Fig. 16) of Mr Laidlay's position when addressing the ball are given. The overlapping of the fingers in the grip of the club, shown in Fig. 15, is, it may be noted, peculiar. Mr Laidlay and J H Taylor, the present champion, are the only two players I know of whose fingers overlap in this manner. When writing on the subject of stance, I cannot refrain from stating the opinion that although too much stress cannot be laid upon the necessity for a good stance, it is frivolous to endeavour to take up exactly the same position as some celebrated player, or even to take up exactly the same position for every drive. Speaking for myself – and I am confident that I am expressing at the same time the views of brother professionals – I take up a stance which is always the same in character, and from which I feel, as I address the ball, that I can hit it; but I never think of the distance one foot is from the other, or how much the right foot is advanced, or the distance the ball may be to the right or left of any particular spot, although I am conscious that these distances are not always precisely the same. Like other players, I have to humour myself and the game in this matter, and I cannot think of a surer way of courting foozles than that of worrying about getting into exactly the same position for each stroke.

I have not yet referred to the position of the legs. Fig. 12 will show that I stand with my legs straight, but just eased at the knees, and the body erect; but it is more usual, and equally good, to see the legs slightly more bent at the knees. I repeat again that the whole position must be easy and comfortable, and not stiff or awkward.

The position above given, it has already been pointed out, is that for driving or playing the long game. In approaching and putting some variations are necessary, and will be referred to in the proper places, viz. in the chapters dealing with these subjects. I call the changes in position which will be described 'variations,' because I do not regard them as being of sufficient importance in character to make them actually different stances.

There have now been described the grip, the position of the ball, and the stance, and the only remaining subject to be dealt with in this chapter is the swing. One speaks of striking the ball, but this scarcely conveys an accurate idea of what is required to be done in playing golf. No doubt the ball is struck, but the stroke should be as little as possible of an up and down motion, and should be of such a nature that the ball

FIG. 17 – THE DRIVE – THE TOP OF THE SWING

is swept away in the course of the swing. The ball is not to be hit as if it were desired to drive it into the ground. The player should rather have in view to swing his club as if to drive something through the ball from behind in the intended line of its flight. What is required is a sharp, quick hit, with a sweeping motion, not a heavy, ponderous stroke. It is the rapidity of the downward swing that propels the ball, and the greater the velocity with which the club-head is travelling at the moment of impact, the greater will be the distance driven. A good swing is as graceful a position as is to be seen in any sport. It is desirable to have as long a swing – that is to say, to have the club-head travelling in as large a circle – as possible, because the club gathers speed as it descends, and the further it has to travel the greater will be its velocity. This is what makes a half swing objectionable; but it is nevertheless possible to have too long a swing, as, for instance, when the club is swung so far back that the player loses control over it. When this happens, there is bound to be a loss of force, and such a swing is less effective than a shorter one.

And now to describe the swing. The player, grasping the club in manner before indicated, and standing in the position before pointed out, will have his arms, slightly bent at the elbows, hanging down in front of the centre of his body, his right shoulder slightly depressed, his body just a little bent forward from the hips, and his knees relaxed, all to such an extent only as will give ease to his position. It may be stated that Mr Laidlay holds his arms not opposite the centre of his body, but somewhat to the left, and this is a natural consequent of his style of play. The player must now swing the club up over his neck or top of his right shoulder until the club-shaft is at right angles with his body, or is across, but not touching, the top of his shoulders. Fig. 17 shows the position at the top of the swing. It has already been said that the club must not be swung with an up and down motion, but with a sweep; and, to carry this into practice, the club-head must be swept back along the ground as far as the arms will permit, until it begins to rise towards the shoulder, the arms being allowed to go well out from the body with the swing, and, as the club rises, the elbows and wrists bending, the shoulders turning round so far as is necessary, and the body easing at the hip- and knee-joints, the left knee turning inward, and the left heel rising off the ground as much as is required to facilitate the swinging round of the club. The right elbow should be kept in to the right side until it is carried out in the course of the swing, but it should not be allowed to rise above the shoulder, even at the top of the swing. Fig. 10 shows the position the right arm should be in at the top of the swing. I may repeat that the grip of the club must be eased, as before pointed out, as the club travels round. I have recommended that the club be swung until it is in a horizontal position across the top of the shoulders; if, however, the swing can be continued beyond this until the club-head dips, good and well, but if it be felt that going further round than is above indicated tends to allow command over the club to be lost, the swing should not be carried further. The turning of the shoulders, the easing of the body at the hip- and knee-joints, and the raising of the left heel off the ground should not be more than is sufficient to enable the club to be swung round with comfort. Attention has been drawn to the position of the right arm at the top (or the full extent backwards) of the swing, and it has been stated that the elbow should be held in to the side until the raising of the club carries it up; the raising of the arm should follow the club in its upward motion, and should not precede it. If the arm be raised and followed by the club, the result is that the whole of the right arm is brought into such a position that the joints jam, and prevent the swing of the club being carried round in manner above directed.

This is the upward part of the swing. In making it the body should not be inclined to the right side; the backbone should be kept steady, and should form, as it were, a pivot round which the shoulders and body turn as far as is required for the easy accomplishment of the swing; the head should be kept as steady as possible, and the action of the shoulders, arms, wrists, and legs should be merely with the view of allowing the club to go round, and not a primary part of the swing. These parts of the body should, so to speak, be carried round by the club, and the movement of them should in no case be precedent to, but should follow, the club. It is too common to see the swing begun by raising the left heel off the ground; this is beginning at the wrong end.

The downward part of the swing is an exact reversal of the upward motion. As the club comes down, the whole position of the player reverts to that from which he originally began the upward swing, until the point is reached from whence it began (at which, or immediately after which, the ball is struck), and the downward swing is thereafter continued in what is technically termed the follow-through – that is, a new upward swing in continuation of the downward is commenced over the left shoulder to a certain extent. This upward swing over the left shoulder – or follow-through – is the exact converse of the upward swing over the right shoulder, the player's body turning in the course of the follow-through till he faces the direction in which the ball is driven. The club-head, arms, and body

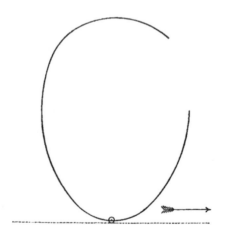

FIG. 18 – THE KIND OF SWING THAT IS NOT DESIRABLE – TOO UP AND DOWN

(The line represents the curve desribed by the club-head)

FIG. 19 – THE DRIVE – THE END OF THE SWING

should be thrown out or follow on in the direction in which the ball is driven, and in the course of this there will be the same easing of the body at the hip- and knee-joints, but exactly the converse of what has been before stated, and the heel of the right foot will be raised off the ground. Fig. 19 shows the end of the swing. A good follow-through is essential to play-

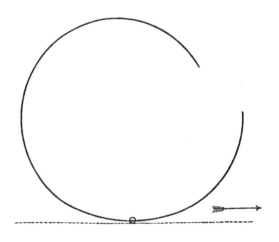

FIG. 20 – THE PROPER KIND OF SWING, VIZ. ONE THAT WILL
SWEEP THE BALL AWAY
(The line represents the curve described by the club-head)

ing a powerful long game; it prevents the ball being undercut, helps to give it a longer flight, and, most important of all, it ensures straight driving; because, when the follow-through is properly carried out, the club-head travels after the ball in the same line in which it is intended to be driven. My father, William Park, senior, who, it is well known, was one of the straightest and longest drivers of his day, carried out the principle of the follow-through to such an extent that he used frequently to run a yard or two after his drive. It has been urged that, in the upward swing, the club-head should be swept back along the ground as far as possible. The reason for this is that in the downward swing the club-head will instinctively be made to travel over the corresponding line that it has traversed in the upward swing; and it is one of the greatest elements in long and straight driving that the club-head should travel in the intended line of flight of the ball as long as possible. The annexed diagrams (Figs. 18 and 20) will give a better idea of my meaning. To illustrate the point more forcibly they are somewhat exaggerated, but the exaggeration helps to show what I mean. The circles do not show the full extent of the follow-through, but are broken off about halfway up.

With the view of making the club-head travel longer in the line of intended flight, some golfers, instead of keeping the body steady and pivoting the shoulders round the backbone, sway themselves towards the right as the club goes up, recovering their original position as it comes down. Theoretically this should improve the swing, but, practically, experience teaches that anything gained by so doing is counterbalanced by (1) the slowness of the movement of the body, and (2) the inaccuracy entailed, and consequent difficulty of hitting the ball truly, which is the essence of perfect and steady play.

Although for the sake of being explicit the swing has been divided into upward and downward, it must not be supposed that there is to be any pause between these two parts; the whole swing from the beginning of the upward raising of the club to the end of the follow-through after the downward sweep should be one easy, smooth, rhythmical motion, without any jerking, and without being dislocated or cramped in any part. The club should be swung backward at a good speed, but without jerking and without undue rapidity, and at the end of the upward swing the downward should be immediately commenced without pause, the downward speed increasing in rapidity until the ball is struck. I believe that a great number of faulty styles of golf arise from the fact that there is an effort made to put force into the downward swing from the moment of its commencement. This, I think, is a mis-

FIG. 21 — A SWING ROUND THE HEAD — TOO HIGH

FIG. 22 — A SWING ROUND THE BODY — TOO LOW

take, as the club should gather speed, and consequently force, as it descends, the greatest amount of force being put into the stroke just before impact with the ball – say within a foot or two of it. As the club comes downward the player will feel his wrists straightening, and this is the most crucial part of the swing. If he wishes to drive well he must get his wrists into the stroke, and give the ball a sharp click just as it is struck. A writer on the game assiduously teaches that the club should be taken back slowly. 'Slow back' is his motto for golfers. With all deference to his opinion, I do not think that this style is one which can be adopted with benefit. Some of our best players have had very quick swings, but none of them at any stage of their career have to my knowledge had a slow back style. I believe that in the swing, as in most else connected with the game, there is virtue in keeping to the middle course. It may be argued that professional teachers of the game tell their pupils to take the club back slowly; but this, it will be found, really amounts in their case to an injunction not to jerk the swing.

It is not possible for me to catalogue the various bad habits into which golfers fall. I can only warn my readers against one or two of the more common faults, and point out what appears to me to be the correct style. In addition to the defects incidentally alluded to in the course of this chapter, there are two into which young players are more than usually prone to fall, and against which I desire to warn them. One is bending the body from the waist in the act of swinging. When the club goes up they pull themselves into an erect position, and when it comes down they bend forward. The player who does that will nine times out of ten miss the ball: it is absolutely fatal to accuracy. The other is moving the position of the feet on the ground in the act of swinging. It is equally fatal to accuracy. I do not refer to raising the heel of the foot off the ground, but to an actual change in the position of one or other foot or both. These errors are the stumbling-blocks of a great many young players.

There still remains to be pointed out an important difference in regard to swings. If a number of golfers be carefully

FIG. 23 – BADLY SLICED

observed, it will be seen that some swing the club round their heads, some round their shoulders, and others round their bodies (see Figs. 21, 17, and 22). The majority of players adopt the second-mentioned style – that is to say, when the top of their swing is reached, if they then paused, the club would be found to lie across their shoulders. Similarly with the others: the club would be found higher up or lower down, depending upon whether the swing was a high one or a low one. Players with differences of this kind may all be equally good golfers. But what is the effect of these differences? The circle described by the club is probably the same in each case, but in the case of the swing round the body it is a circle less perpendicular or more laid on its side than is the case in the swing round the shoulders. It therefore appears that it is more likely to pull or slice the ball than is the more perpendicular circle or swing, and the lesson to be derived from all this is to play with as upright a swing as is consistent with fair hitting. With a very upright swing, such as round the head (Fig. 21), there is some danger of a twist creeping into the style, which must of course be avoided. It is not possible to have an absolutely perpendicular swing, nor, as above pointed out, is it desirable. It will be remembered that the nearer a golfer stands to the ball, and the more upright a club he uses, the more perpendicular must be his swing.

In swinging the club it should not at any part of the swing touch the body. I know players who invariably touch their shoulders at the top of the swing, so much so that their club-shafts thereby become bent; but this is a very bad habit, and should be discouraged. It is scarcely possible to contract a worse fault; the touch with the body puts the whole mechanism out of joint.

An error golfers sometimes fall into unconsciously is that of lifting the club quickly up at the end of the downward swing, and throwing the body over to the right, instead of following through. The result of this is that the ball is 'whipped up' and driven into the air. Some players are unable to cure themselves of the habit, and endeavour to counteract the effect by teeing the ball towards the right foot. This, no doubt, helps to lessen the evil; but it is better to break oneself of the bad habit, and cultivate a follow-through.

Slicing the ball is caused in most cases by a fault of swing, the fault in this case lying in drawing the arms in towards the body, instead of following through (Fig. 23). Slicing appears to impart two motions to the ball. The face of the club at the moment of impact is travelling forward; but it is also, owing to the drawing in of the arms, travelling across the ball from right to left, and the result of the two motions is that the ball is propelled forward with a spin upon it, and whenever the forward motion is to any extent exhausted, the spin takes effect and causes the ball to circle to the right. Pulling or hooking may be caused by turning the body round at the end of the swing, after the fashion of a man using a scythe, or by pulling round the left arm, or by turning in the nose of the club as it hits the ball. Here, again, a spin is put upon the ball, making it circle to the left. If the arms are thrown well out after the swing, neither slicing nor pulling can take place, and the ball is driven with a forward motion without side spin.

The face of the club should not be hung over the ball. It is a fault which some players who drive off the left leg have. They hold their hands too much to the left of their bodies, thus making the face of the club lie over the ball. No doubt if the stroke is got away the ball is kept down and not driven high, but the more usual effect is to founder the shot.

After taking up the stance, it is usual to rest the head of the club for a moment behind the ball, and then give it a preliminary waggle over the ball. The resting of the club allows a better aim to be taken for the stroke; but care must be taken that the rule in regard to improving the lie, except in the case of teed shots, is not infringed. The object of the waggle is to make sure that the club and arms are free; it is, in short, a sort of trial swing, or, as it has been aptly termed, a preliminary canter before entering upon the race. It is better to take a slow, sweeping waggle than a quick, jerky one, and it should be done with the wrists only. The waggle should be of the briefest possible duration, as it is always a mistake to hang over a stroke. At the same time, the waggle is not unnecessary, as it steadies the player before actually making the stroke.

The ball should be hit with the centre of the face of the club. The maker's name is a good guide for the point of impact. If hit near the heel of the club the ball will go straight a certain distance, and then curve round to the right in the same way as if it had been sliced, and if it be hit near the toe of the club the stroke will likely be pulled.

Some players always aim at the ball with the extreme toe of the club, and while swinging fall forward with their bodies, so that the ball is accurately hit. This is a serious fault, and one which grows alarmingly; and though possibly one may not feel the effect at the time, he should instantly discourage such tendency, as he may afterwards find his play seriously affected, and the habit more difficult to break through.

In playing with iron clubs it will be found advisable to take a somewhat shorter swing, and to grasp the club more firmly.

It is perhaps scarcely necessary to say that the essential and elementary principle in all golf is, Keep your eye on the ball. This rule has been refined to the extent of saying, Keep your eye on the exact spot of the ball you intend to hit – that is, behind the ball; but doing so seems to add a needless complexity to an otherwise simple rule.

In concluding this chapter I will summarise the actions usual to playing: Having taken up the proper stance (in doing this, do not fiddle about with the feet over much), and got the right grip of the club, both of which will soon become instinctive, rest the club-head behind the ball for a moment, to make sure that the ball is within reach; waggle the club over the ball once or twice; again rest the club-head behind the ball for an instant, and swing.

CHAPTER FOUR

The Long Game

THE EXPRESSION 'THE LONG GAME' is applied to driving, or strokes off the tee, and to play through the green, or the intermediate strokes between the drive and the approach to the hole, with the exception of play out of hazards. It is fairly descriptive of the nature of this part of the game, in which the object is to propel the ball as far as possible with each stroke. It can hardly be denied by any one who has played golf, that of all the different parts of the game none gives greater pleasure than long driving, although accurate approaching and putting conduce more to the winning of matches and low scoring. The golfer who does not feel a sensation of keen gratification, of superiority of power and skill, invest his whole body when he gets away a long straight drive, must indeed be unimpressionable. After years of play I still am able, and hope that I shall always be, to experience such feelings. One is told of miraculous drives of 300 yards and upwards; indeed, drives are spoken of as if anything short of that figure were hardly worthy of notice. Although I can drive 'as far as my neighbours, and whiles a bit further,' I frankly say that I cannot, and never could, drive 300 yards, and I am convinced that no man can, unless under exceptionally favourable circumstances. An extraordinarily long shot may be made now and again, but experience proves that 200 yards is about the average limit of really long driving; 170 or 180 yards may be considered first-class, and anything over 150 yards is fairly good.

Reference is made to the second chapter, in which suggestions are given with the view of aiding in the selection of clubs. In addition to what is there stated, it may be added that a driver with a fairly stiff shaft will be found the most useful. A club with a supple shaft may possibly drive a longer ball with greater ease, but it renders the play very much more unsteady, and against a head or a cross wind there is an increased risk of pulling or slicing. Erratic driving counterbalances, on the wrong side, any advantage in extra length of stroke obtained by using a supple club, and therefore a golfer will never regret his driver being somewhat stiff. If, however, he insists upon having a supple shaft, the best advice that can be given to him is to swing easily, and, above everything, refrain from jerking, as his club will not permit of liberties being used.

For foozled drives less excuse can be offered than for any other mistakes. In the case of the drive alone, with a single exception applicable to play in medal competitions, every opportunity is afforded for making a perfect stroke. Within the limits of the teeing-ground the position from which the ball is to be struck can be selected, and a tee used with the object of permitting the best possible stroke to be taken. If, therefore, a mistake is made, the player has himself, and himself only, to blame. The importance of getting away a good drive at each hole can hardly be overrated. What are the respective positions of one golfer who has got away a 'screamer' for a tee-shot and of another who has topped his ball? The first feels elated and confident, and able for almost anything, and besides, his ball is about a couple of hundred yards nearer the hole than when he started; the latter feels dejected, and has to play the long odds to his opponent, and indeed may consider himself lucky if he has not to extricate his ball from a hazard and then play the two more. A few topped or duffed tee-shots will break down any but the most determined and hardened of players. When a mistake is made in another part of the game, one can persuade himself that it arose through a bad lie, or can offer one or other of the numerous excuses that readily occur; but a foozled drive cannot be explained away in any such fashion. Something may be blamed; but, all the same, the fault in reality lay with the player himself – for was not the tee his own choice? – and self-deceit under such circumstances is not an easy matter.

The selection of a tee is a detail by no means to be

despised; it is seldom left to a caddie, and not only do all golfers select their own tees, but many of them prefer to tee their own balls. If possible, a place should be chosen where there is a slight rise in the direction of the drive, the object being to get a clear space behind the ball for the free swing of the club. The stance should be a firm, comfortable one, and on the same level as the ball, neither higher nor lower. It is preferable to tee upon grass if possible; the sight of bare earth is apt to lead to topping, as it looks hard, and gives the impression that contact between it and the club-head, which might happen with a sclaffy shot, would inevitably result in damage to the club; consequently the player intuitively does not allow the club to get down as it ought. I rather favour a high tee; if a deep-faced club be used, there is not much danger of getting too far below the ball and undercutting it. By this I do not wish it to be understood that a small mountain is to be made for a tee; but the ball should be well raised, say about half an inch off the surface of the ground. If driving against a head wind, a lower tee may be taken with the view of keeping the ball from rising too high. The best method of making a tee is to take a sufficient quantity of sand – a comparatively small pinch will suffice – form it with the fingers and thumb into a cone on the selected spot, and then press down with the palm of the hand. The ball should be lightly placed on the top of this, and not imbedded in it. One frequently sees a whole handful of sand laid down and the ball firmly buried in the centre. From such a tee the proper club to be used is a niblick; it is the best implement for extracting the ball from the bunker – I can call it nothing else – so formed. Some few players do not use a tee at all; they prefer simply to lay the ball on the ground. I think, however, that it is better to take advantage of the privilege of teeing.

If, in the course of the preliminary waggle, or in drawing back the club in the act of swinging, it happens to touch the ground behind the ball, it will invariably be advisable to change the tee; such a touch indicates that a suitable spot has not been chosen. But even if the tee be unexceptionable, the

FIG. 24 – A GOOD TEE   FIG. 25 – A BAD TEE

mere fact of having hit the ground will disturb the accuracy of aim, and tend to put the player off his drive. When it is permissible to do so according to the rules, anything that is apt to catch the eye or interfere with the club in the course of the swing, or with the flight of the ball as it rises, should be removed.

Hitherto the subject dealt with in this chapter has been confined exclusively to driving or tee-shots. Play through the green is fully deserving of as much attention, and is more difficult than driving, because in it a greater variety of strokes is to be found. With the exception of those cases specified in the rules, the ball must always be played as it lies; and here is introduced an element of chance, for the stroke to a great extent depends upon the lie. It frequently happens that, after two equally fine drives, the ball in one case will be found lying as well as if teed, in such a position that a good swipe at it can be got with a play-club, while in the other it may be lying so badly as to require to be played with an iron club. Such an occurrence is purely luck, and will happen on the best of greens; it is one of the elements of golf, and although aggravating enough at the time to him who experiences the worst side of it, the luck will, generally speaking, be found to be pretty evenly divided.

It will be obvious that, as the ball cannot be placed to suit the player, he must take up his stance relatively to it, getting into the position indicated in the preceding chapter.

When one reaches the ball after a drive, the question that naturally arises first is, What club should be used? The answer to this depends upon two things, viz. the distance to the hole and the lie of the ball. In play through the green it is presupposed that the distance is sufficient to admit of a full shot with any club; strokes which will lay the ball on the green are generally termed approaches, and will be treated of under that head. It may therefore be stated that the chief factor in determining the club to be used is the lie of the ball. For a good-lying ball the proper club is a driver, because the desired object is to get the greatest possible distance out of the stroke, and for this purpose the driver is unequalled. Even if the ball be not lying quite clear, an experienced player will take his driver and get away a long shot; but many of the best golfers habitually use a brassy or spoon, and there is little doubt that for such a purpose they are the more reliable clubs. I therefore recommend a brassy – spoons not being so frequently carried – for all play through the green. This on the principle that it is better to play steadily with a brassy than to use a driver, with the possible result of obtaining one good stroke, further in distance than can be got with a brassy, and three or four indifferent ones. The stiffness of the brassy shaft and the loft on the face are both in favour of that club, as opposed to a driver, for such strokes.

Among the variety of lies in which the ball may be found is that termed 'a cupped ball.' This expression is applied to a ball lying in a shallow hollow, such as may have been made by some former player having cut out a piece of turf. Unless the cup is very shallow – in which case an experienced golfer may use his driver if he prefers – the proper club for such a stroke is a brassy, for two reasons: first, because the small head allows of its fitting into the cup; and second, because the loft on the face makes the ball rise more quickly. A cupped ball gives room for playing one of the finest strokes in golf. A ball ought to be driven nearly as far out of a cup as off a tee; but, instead, how often is the stroke miserably foozled! To play a cupped ball successfully great accuracy of aim is required, and the club must be swung with less of a sweep than in playing tee-shots – coming down straighter to the ball, and jerking it out of the cup; as a result, after the ball is struck the club-head catches in the ground and cuts the turf. It is to be borne in mind that, if the stroke is to be successful, the ball must be struck, and struck clean, before the turf is touched; the cutting of the turf is to come after the ball is away, and is a consequent of the swing being intercepted. If the turf be first cut, and the ball afterwards struck, the entire force will be taken out of the stroke before the ball is reached. When the ball lies clear on the green, it must be apparent that the bottom of the club should sweep over the surface; but, as happens in the case of a cupped ball, when the ball is slightly under the level of the surrounding ground, the swing must be correspondingly lowered, so that the sole of the club will be below the centre of the ball. Not only must the swing be lowered, but the stroke must be played somewhat as if it were intended to drive the ball down, and hence the club-head is bound to hit the ground in front of where the ball lay. The swing cannot be the same as in the case of a teed ball; because, if the stroke be played with the same sweep, one of two things must obviously happen: either the ground at the back of the ball will be struck first, in which case the whole force will be expended before the ball is touched; or, the ball being below the surface of the ground in the cup, it will be topped. The swing must therefore be modified so that the club will not sweep the ground, but will come down between the ball and the edge of the cup behind it, thus entailing, as is above explained, a more up and down swing. The annexed diagram will show more clearly what I mean. The hard line shows the circle which the club-head will follow, and the dotted line shows the circle it would follow if the ball lay clear and not cupped. With the view of aiding in the 'picking up' of a cupped hall, it is well to stand somewhat over it – that is to say, to keep the ball nearer the right foot than would be done in playing a tee stroke. If the cup be anything deep, it may not be possible to use a brassy, in which case a cleek or driving-mashie, or even an iron, may be required to get the ball away. On soft greens the yielding nature of the turf renders it possible to get away a deep-lying ball, which would be almost unplayable on hard ground. A ball lying so deep as to require the use of an iron can scarcely be said to be cupped; it really lies in a hole, and if the hole is deep, it may not be possible to do more than extricate the ball, in which case a mashie or a niblick will probably be the best club to take. There should not, however, be any holes of this description on a green in the line of play.

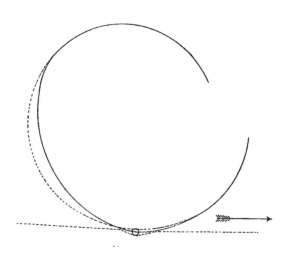

FIG. 26 – A CUPPED BALL

A heavy-lying ball is frequently got on inland courses – that is, a ball lying more or less imbedded in grass or rushes. For such a lie a brassy or a cleek should be used, unless the ball be actually buried, when an iron may be the best club. A driving-mashie is excellent for all heavy lies, as the small head minimises the loss of force through contact with surrounding obstructions, and its deep face lessens the danger which always exists of cutting in below the ball, and causing it to jump up into the air instead of being driven forward. The secret of playing such strokes well lies in accurate hitting and playing with jerk. The reason for the jerk in these cases is that if the usual sweeping swing be taken the club will catch in the grass or rushes before it reaches the ball, and a great part of the force will be taken out of the stroke.

In a preceding part of this chapter I have cautioned golfers against jerking their swing, and this must not be confounded with the jerk necessary in playing cupped and heavy-lying balls. In the former case it is the swing that is jerked, owing to excessive force being put into it suddenly at any particular stage; in the latter the swing is smooth and easy – it is the ball that is jerked out of its lie.

On links where the ground is uneven and hummocky, a ball will often be found lying at the back of one of these little hillocks. It is hardly necessary to point out that if the ball is driven into the hillock all the force will be taken out of the stroke, and the ball will bound into the air and travel a comparatively short distance thereafter. It is therefore necessary to use a club with sufficient loft to make the ball clear the obstruction. A sliced ball will rise more quickly, but of course its flight will be deflected off the straight course, and due allowance must be made therefore.

A hanging ball – that is, a ball lying on ground sloping downward in the direction of play – frequently occurs, and it is surprising how few golfers are able to play it with any degree of success. A brassy or spoon is the appropriate club, the desideratum being loft on the face. The mistake usually made is trying to do something that will aid in lofting the ball. Such an effort is entirely unnecessary, and is the very thing that ruins nine-tenths of these strokes. All that is required is to play the ball as if it lay on a level surface, and leave the rest to the loft on the face of the club. Provided a club be used with sufficient loft, there is no fear of the stroke failing. It is possible, too, to get the ball lying on the side of a hillock, so that the ball is in one case below the spot where the player stands, and in the other case above it. In such cases it is necessary that extreme care be taken to make absolutely sure of hitting the ball truly. In the first case, however truly the ball is struck, there is a tendency, from the position in which the player must stand, to slice; and in the other case there is, for a similar reason, a tendency to pull. Sometimes a perfectly straight shot will be got away, but it is well to allow for slicing or pulling.

It occasionally happens on greens where there are walls or fences, that the ball may be found lying up against them, so close that there is danger of hitting them. It is to be kept in view that the ball will travel in the direction in which the club-face looks, or at right angles to the line of the face; and hence, if the nose of the club be held in so that the face looks slightly away from the wall or fence, it may be possible to drive the ball in that direction. A good deal of nerve is required to play such a stroke successfully, as the proximity of the obstacle is always suggestive of prospective damage to the club. When the ball lies close to a wall or fence, and it is desired to play it out at right angles, it may sometimes be found impossible to swing the club even sufficiently to enable a wrist stroke to be taken. In such eases I have seen a stroke cleverly made by the player facing the wall, straddling his legs, and playing the ball through between them, stooping down and grasping the club very short. It is a stroke quite worth trying in a tight position.

The causes of slicing, heeling, pulling, and hooking have been explained before. As will hereafter be pointed out, experienced golfers occasionally heel and pull intentionally when they consider themselves justified in running risks to obtain a probable advantage. To pull, the club must be swung with a scythe-like movement, or the left arm pulled round. It is not usual, and not a good practice, either to slice or hook intentionally, because the shot will probably be a very wild one. The difficulty, however, with which most players have to contend is not how to put on heel or pull, but how to cure the persistent habit of getting a spin on the ball unconsciously. Many golfers are hardly able to play a straight shot, and instead of being an aid, as it may occasionally be, it becomes a serious drawback. As already stated, the cultivation of a proper swing and follow-through is the cure, and the only real one, for all these faults. I have heard it recommended to stand nearer the ball for pulling and hooking and further away for slicing and heeling, and the opposite advice in each case has also been given; but the faults cannot be cured by either of these devices. They, in fact, only increase the evil; and though there may be an apparent improvement at the time, the old fault will reappear, possibly in an aggravated form, until the defective swing, which is the root of the trouble, has been displaced by one modelled on the orthodox lines.

Topping and sclaffing are other evils that dog the golfer, the first consisting in not getting down sufficiently to the ball, and the other in getting down too far. These faults generally arise from taking the eye off the ball. Keep the eye on the ball seems a simple enough precept to act up to, but there is an irresistible desire in the untutored golfer to allow his eye to wander off the ball before it is struck, and to glance in the direction of its intended flight. The only remedy is to rigidly obey the rule, and not permit the eye to leave the ball until it is struck. Topping and sclaffing may also be the result of playing with too short or too long a club. A golfer, when he is aware that the fault may arise from this cause, should have no difficulty in determining whether in his case it is due to the club or not.

Golfers cannot be too carefully cautioned against pressing; it is an insidious habit that creeps into the game in playing against a stronger opponent. Pressing is very often supposed to consist of putting extra force into a stroke; but, to my mind, this definition is not strictly accurate, as I do not think that the mere fact of using extra force will spoil any stroke, provided the force be put in gradually. The evil of pressing consists in the force being exerted suddenly and with visible effort in the course of the downward swing. I do not in any, unless exceptional cases – as, for instance, when a very long stroke is absolutely necessary – recommend putting extra force into a stroke. The more easily the club is swung, the less likelihood is there of mistakes being made. At the same time, if a ball is to be driven any distance it must be hit, and hit hard, and the golfer who merely lets the club descend on the ball without putting pith into the swing will never drive a long ball, and will never rank as a class player; but, beyond the amount of force usually employed, he should under ordinary circumstances never go. Unless required by the character of the lie of the ball, he should not play with jerk. As before explained, the jerk makes the swing more up and down, and is designed to slip the club-head in between the ball and some obstruction behind it: this is not applicable in the case of a clear-lying ball. Where it is at all possible, the ball should be swept away, as explained in the chapter describing the swing.

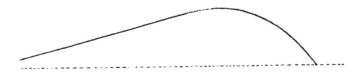

FIG. 27 – A GOOD DRIVE

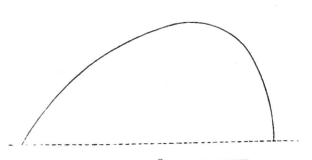

FIG. 28 – A BAD DRIVE

With a bad-lying ball it is a common error, more especially among inexperienced players, to imagine that the difficulty is to be overcome by using brute force, and this force is exercised in pressing. A more fatal mistake cannot be made. Golf is not a game of force; it is a game of skill, and every stroke is more or less of a delicate nature, as are the implements employed in the play of it. Pressing disturbs the accuracy of aim – the all-important part – and a miserable foozle is the result. Great accuracy is the essence of the successful negotiation of a difficult stroke, whether caused by a bad lie or otherwise, and to ensure this the swing must be easy. By using a short club, or taking a shorter grip, more command over it can be obtained, and the grip should be firmer with both hands to prevent its being turned by contact with an obstruction or with the ground. Putting on a little slice or cut is of great assistance in enabling the ball to get away; but, as before explained, allowance must be made for deflection in the direction of the drive.

A well hit drive should be almost all carry; the ball should not run any distance after it falls, and should go away low and rise gradually, as shown in Fig. 27. If it goes away high at first (Fig. 28), it is a pretty good sign that it has been undercut. Undercut and the remedy have been before explained.

CHAPTER FIVE

Approaching

THE TERM APPROACH, in its strictest sense, is applied to any stroke which is intended to lay the ball on the putting-green. It is not, however, applied to a teed shot which reaches the green at a short hole, and it is seldom applied at long holes to full strokes from any wooden club (except a baffy or short-spoon) which place the ball on the green. Although approaching includes full strokes with a cleek, iron, mashie, baffy, or short-spoon, it applies more particularly to three-quarter, half, or wrist shots. These expressions do not convey to every mind their actual meaning. The uninitiated are apt to suppose that the words three-quarter and half refer to the distance the ball is driven; thus a three-quarter and a half stroke would respectively mean a stroke which drives the ball three-quarters or half the distance of a full shot. This, of course, is not the case, as a half stroke can be driven by a player possessed of powerful wrists and arms very nearly as far as a full shot. The expressions apply to the extent of the swing. Thus, in a three-quarter stroke, the club is swung back about three-quarters the distance it would be for a full stroke, and similarly with a half stroke. The term wrist stroke is much more correct in its description; it means exactly what it says, viz. a stroke played with the wrists. It must be obvious that with different players the distances represented by full, three-quarter, and half strokes will vary considerably. One man may drive even further with a half stroke than another will with a full shot, and it is thus impossible to lay down any rule in regard to when a wrist, or a half, or a three-quarter stroke should be played. Every golfer must find out his own strength, and play accordingly.

The approach is the most difficult, and sometimes the

most delicate, stroke in the whole game. In driving and play through the green the object to be attained is to drive the ball as far as possible, and the one thing to do is to hit the ball, and hit it as hard as the golfer dare risk. In approaching, not only must the ball be hit truly, but the distance to the hole must be calculated and the force employed proportioned thereto, and consideration must be given to the nature of the ground to determine whether the ball is to be lofted or run up. These considerations make the stroke more complex. But in no part of the game is there afforded a greater opportunity for the display of skill, as opposed to force, than in this, and nowhere is skill better repaid. For at every hole the player who can lay his approach near the flag has the chance of saving a stroke off his less skilful adversary, provided he does not, by indifferent putting, throw away the advantage so gained.

When the putting-green is so far distant that a full shot is required, be it with a cleek, a spoon, or an iron, there is no difference between the manner of playing such a stroke and a similarly lying ball through the green, due regard being always had to the distance to be traversed. I would only repeat that, in using a cleek or any other iron club, it must be held firmly, and the ball struck sharply. Three-quarter and half strokes are to my mind much more difficult to play than full shots, especially the former. There is always a disposition to jerk the swing, as if to compensate for its being shortened, and this generally results in topping the ball. It is not safe to attempt to play anything under a full shot with any wooden club save a baffy or a short spoon, which, from their stiffness of shaft, may be used equally as well as a cleek or iron; but a club with a supple shaft cannot be used without the greatest danger of foozling. There cannot be any possible reason for pressing a half or three-quarter stroke, because, if it is desired to drive the ball further, the proper course is to lengthen the swing and take a full shot. Therefore, in playing these strokes, there should not, under any circumstances, be pressing: swing easily.

With regard to three-quarter strokes, although the term is

still kept up, the necessity for playing them has almost, if not entirely, disappeared. In the older days of golf, spoons, cleeks, and irons were respectively made with a recognised amount of loft on each, and it frequently happened that a three-quarter stroke was absolutely necessary to lay the ball near the hole. Nowadays spoons have almost disappeared, their place being taken by cleeks having varying amounts of pitch on the face; and irons are made with almost any degree of pitch – they may be almost flat-faced, as in driving-irons, or may have a very great amount of loft, as in the case of pitching-irons. When a golfer states that he played a certain stroke with his iron, one cannot judge whether it was a remarkable stroke or not till the iron used has been examined. This multiplication of cleeks and irons has almost entirely eliminated the three-quarter stroke from golf; because, by a judicious selection of one or two extra clubs, it is possible to have a club at hand a full or half shot from which will come in place of the three-quarter stroke. A full stroke is by far the easiest to play, and a half shot is infinitely less difficult than a three-quarter one. For these reasons I do not propose to go further into detail than I have done as to the play of three-quarter strokes.

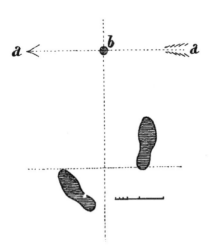

FIG. 29 – THE APPROACH – DIAGRAM OF POSITION

The position of the ball and stance for playing half shots is somewhat, though not materially, different from that before described. As in the former case, an illustration (Fig. 30) and a diagram (Fig. 29) are given. The ball is nearer the player's body, and nearer also to the line of the right foot. The right foot is also further advanced. Fig. 31 shows the top of the swing. It need hardly be pointed out that, as the club is not swung far round, the shoulders and body do not move so much as in playing a full stroke. The shoulders must move round, and the body must be eased (as is pointed out in the chapter on style) to a certain extent, it is true, but the less they do so the better, consistently with letting the club go sufficiently round. The left foot will be just raised off the heel and nothing more, the left leg being flexed to ease the swing. It may, in fact, be said that the feet should not, if possible, be moved at all. The elbow of the right arm should be kept in to the body and not allowed to rise, but all the same the arms will be thrown out just as in playing full strokes. The follow-through will take place at the end of the swing; but instead of throwing the club and arms after the ball, they will rise quicker, and continue upwards over the left shoulder more than in the direction of the flight of the ball.

Some golfers can drive a very long ball with a half swing; but the half swing used in such a case is hardly the half swing desirable for playing approaches. This half swing is more of the character of a very long sweep along the ground succeeded by a good follow-through; and although the club may not be taken so far round the shoulders as in a full swing, the distance actually traversed by the club-head will not be much less, and, being a sweep, it gives a great amount of forward propulsion to the ball.

Of wrist strokes there is an infinite variety of gradation – anything less than a half stroke falls under this definition. No further remarks on this subject require to be made, save that the ball should be nearer the player, and the feet closer together. Fig. 32 shows the top of the swing. It will be observed that both legs are slightly more bent at the knees than is the case in

FIG. 30 – THE APPROACH – ADDRESSING THE BALL

FIG. 31 – A HALF SHOT – THE TOP OF THE SWING

FIG. 32 – A WRIST SHOT – THE TOP OF THE SWING

FIG. 33 – CUTTING THE FEET FROM IT – THE TOP OF THE SWING

FIG. 34 – CUTTING THE FEET FROM IT – THE END OF THE SWING

FIG. 35 – THE APPROACH, OFF THE LEFT LEG – MR LAIDLAY
ADDRESSING THE BALL

playing a full shot, and that the body moves very little; in fact, wrist strokes are almost entirely played with the wrists, assisted to a small extent by the arms. I would only add: Stand firmly, and do not move the feet at all; keep the right elbow well in to the side, and play from the wrists, giving the ball a quick, sharp hit.

In all these strokes the club must be held firmly with both hands, to give more command over it, and to prevent its turning. It will be found of material assistance if the club be grasped further down the shaft; and the shorter the distance of the stroke to be played, the shorter a grip of the club may be taken.

In standing according to the directions above given, it will be found that while the weight of the body is supported on both legs, the right really gives the greatest amount of support. This can be easily tested by trying to lift either foot off the ground. For the above reason, this mode of playing approaches has been termed 'off the right leg,' and it is the method most usually adopted. Hereafter an alternative method, termed 'off the left leg,' will be explained.

With the view of making iron approaches fall dead, more especially those played from shorter distances, it has been advocated that they should be played with slice, or cut, as it is more frequently termed in this case. This is done, as before explained, by drawing the arms in towards the body in the act of hitting the ball, and omitting the follow-through. This probably may have the desired effect – and theoretically it is all very well – but practically it is exceedingly difficult to do successfully, and placing the risk of failure against the advantage to be gained, I do not think that in the ordinary case it is worth attempting. I therefore recommend that all approaches be played without slice. If, however, the player has sufficient confidence in his ability to put on the cut, and is desirous of trying it, he will have to keep in view that the effect is to make the ball run to the right-hand side, and he must make allowance for this by playing, not straight on the flag, but to the left of it Personally, I am inclined to think, from the experience I have had, that fewer golfers play approaches with cut than is generally supposed. Any player will readily show how the stroke is done, and may be unwilling to admit that he does not usually play with cut, desiring to have the credit of playing as scientific a game as his neighbours; but watch him when he is playing a match – it will be seen that his professions in this respect are hardly consistent with his practice. It is not difficult to put on cut when a ball is teed or dropped on a fine piece of turf, simply for the purpose of illustrating the stroke; but it is quite a different matter to play approaches in this manner from the multifarious lies – good, bad, and indifferent – that occur in actual play. Slice can only be safely put on in short approaches: in a long approach the effect of it might be to deflect the ball so much that it would not go near the green. In connection with this subject, it may be remarked that, under ordinary circumstances, a ball will not run very far after it lands off anything over a half cleek or a half iron shot. It may run some distance if the ground be hard, or if it shoots off a downward slope, or if the wind be with the ball. In such cases it is not possible to make the ball fall dead by any means.

With wrist shots there is more run on the ball in proportion than with any others, and it may be absolutely necessary to make a wrist shot fall dead, as, for instance, where the hole lies between two bunkers, one in front over which the ball must be pitched, and one behind into which it will certainly roll if there is much run on it. There are other expedients resorted to for this purpose besides putting on cut. One is to lay back the face of the iron. To do this the player must stand in such a position that the ball will be more in a line with his left foot. But this method is no better than using a club with a very great deal of pitch, the difficulty of which will be explained later on; it is therefore not necessary to do more than refer briefly to it in this place. There is another method, known as 'cutting the feet from it,' and this is the most effectual of all, and undoubtedly the proper way of playing the stroke. It is, however, somewhat difficult to play this stroke, and it is still more difficult to describe it. The stance and position are the same as for an ordinary iron approach, and so is the grip. The swing must, however, be much more of an up and down nature than in the ordinary approach, and played sharply. The head of the iron is slipped in between the ball and the turf (not swept over the ground), with the result that a large amount of back spin is imparted to the ball, and in the follow-through the arms are not thrown out in the line of play, but are lifted up straighter, with the object of 'whipping up' the ball. With the view of showing the stroke, two illustrations are given, one of the top of the swing (Fig. 33), and the other of the end of it (Fig. 34). The essence of the stroke lies in hitting the ball smartly and quickly; and the more quickly the ball is hit, the more back spin is put upon it, therefore the higher will it be lofted, and the shorter distance will it travel. If the face of the iron be looked at after playing, it will be found that the mark made on it is not a round mark, such as is made, for example, in playing a full cleek shot; it is a sort of oval smear from the bottom towards the top of the blade, as if the face of the iron had forced itself under the ball before the latter had moved. This, I anticipate, is what actually does happen; and hence, as above stated, the more quickly the stroke is played the more back spin is put on the ball. The stroke will be an utter failure unless the club-head gets well under the ball. On a soft green such a stroke can invariably be played with success; but on a hard green, and out of a bad lie, it is difficult, but not impossible. Such strokes can best be played with a lofting-iron.

The alternative mode of playing approaches is 'off the left leg.' The best exponent of this style is Mr Laidlay, and the illustration (Fig. 35) and diagram (Fig. 36) represent that gentleman's position. In this case the weight of the body is thrown upon the left leg, and the club is held toward the player's left side. Mr Laidlay prefers to play approaches with an iron that has not a great deal of loft on it, thus getting a comparatively low shot, and allowing the ball to finish with a run after the pitch; but for lofted approaches he invariably uses a mashie.

Mr Laidlay believes strongly in what he terms 'shoulder

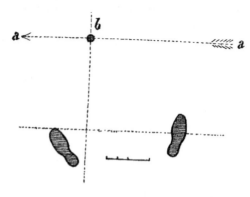

FIG. 36 – THE APPROACH – DIAGRAM OF MR LAIDLAY'S POSITION

shots,' which are similar to the stroke mentioned at page 69. He considers that they are most useful and deadly, especially in a wind, and his opinion on this matter is of great weight. By these shots a long distance can be got out of a cleek or iron without taking a full swing, and hence they are very useful to men who begin golf when up in years.

Every one will easily understand what has already been pointed out, that approach strokes must vary considerably in length, depending upon distance from the putting-green. With regard to long approaches there cannot be much difficulty, because one is tied down to the club that will drive the ball the distance; but in shorter approaches one has a choice of clubs at his command, and on this subject I should like to say a few words. First and foremost, I should not in any case, save for long approaches, recommend the use of a spoon. In former days the baffy was used almost exclusively for all approaches; but why? because it was the only suitable club at the command of golfers in those days. Now that we have cleeks and irons the baffy has disappeared almost entirely. I do not know any present-day golfer of note who uses it regularly. The reason for this principally lies in the fact that more control over the ball is obtained with an iron club. Further, I think that the nearer the ball can be kept to the ground in playing short approaches, the more precision can be obtained. Hence it is better to skiff up a ball with a cleek than to pitch it with an iron. Nay, more, if a putter can be used, don't use a cleek. I am old enough to remember Bob Ferguson of Musselburgh in his best days, and the marvellous precision with which he used to run up his approaches with a putter; and even before Bob Ferguson's day, I remember my father playing the same strokes in the same way, and with the same precision. Using their putters did not spoil either of these golfers in his iron play. Bob Ferguson's iron play at North Berwick, where he used to pitch up balls when he could not run them with his putter, is still fresh in the memory of many. I quote the play of these golfers to show that I am not advocating a theory which has not been tested and proved sound.

Regard must always be had to the nature of the ground between the place where the ball lies and the hole, and upon that will depend the club to be used. If a putter be used, the ball will not, of course, rise at all, but will roll along the ground; if a cleek be used, the ball will rise but a few feet, depending upon the length and consequent strength of the stroke, and will roll a good bit after the pitch is exhausted; while, using the iron, the stroke will be pitched up to the green and roll a comparatively short distance. On a hard green, running up will be found most successful, because it is difficult to pitch a ball dead off an iron, and should it happen to alight on any irregularity it may shoot forward or may bound off in any direction; hence the superiority of running up, because there is much more forward motion on the ball, and it will not, if it hit some irregularity, be deflected to such an extent as if pitched. There is also this advantage, that, the straighter the face of the club, the less is a ball affected when not quite accurately struck, and it is easier to judge the distance – that is to say, an error in calculating the strength tells less against the stroke.

The more pitch there is on a club the less striking surface is presented to the ball, and the more is any mistake magnified. The diagram (Fig. 37) will show more clearly what I mean. A and B represent blades of equal depth of two iron clubs, A having very little pitch and B a good deal. Now, while almost

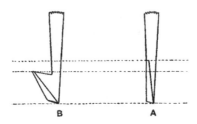

FIG. 37 – THE EFFECT OF PITCH ON IRON CLUBS

the entire surface of A is perpendicular and available for hitting the ball, in the case of B – owing to the pitch – the perpendicular height of the blade when in position for play is reduced to about two-thirds of that of A. This is what makes it difficult to use irons with a great amount of loft.

The iron is undoubtedly the best all-round club for playing approaches, and where the ball requires to be lofted, it, or a similar club, must be used; but this fact does not detract from what I have said above.

On courses where the ground is soft, and possibly the putting-greens are surrounded with rough grass, it is not possible to play cleek or putter approaches – the ball will not run; and in these cases it must be pitched on to the green. On such greens, however, owing to their soft nature, the ball can generally be so played to advantage, and the golfer attempting to use his cleek or putter will be at a corresponding disadvantage owing to the ball catching in the soft ground.

In all approach play remember the motto, 'Be up,' unless there is some good reason to the contrary. It is quite possible, and indeed frequently happens, that an approach may be holed out; but unless it is up, this can never occur.

A golfer should always keep in mind his own strength or weakness, and should never allow false pride to interfere with his play. There is no disgrace, and often not even implied inferiority, in not being able to play so long a cleek shot or so long an iron shot as another man, and he should select the club he is to use in approaching entirely irrespective of the club his opponent or any other player may use. One player may take a half cleek or an iron shot, where another will require a full cleek shot; but the latter should not allow this to deter him from taking a full cleek shot. There is a great temptation to emulate the play of a stronger opponent.

For short approaches a mashie may be used; but it is more difficult to handle than an iron, owing to the smaller size of the head and the amount of pitch.

I do not wish to say anything that can be construed into advocating divots being cut out of links in play, but I believe that it helps to steady an approach, especially when the ball is to be pitched, if a little turf is taken with the stroke. Do not dig deep into the ground, but just take the surface off the turf. It ensures getting under the ball, and lessens the danger of pulling or slicing; but, above all things, see that the turf cut is replaced and firmly trodden down.

CHAPTER SIX

Putting

REFERENCE TO THE rules of the game will show that the putting-green is defined as the ground within twenty yards of the hole, excepting hazards. Putting applies strictly to play upon the putting-green, the strokes themselves being called putts. While this is the strict meaning, the verb to putt is sometimes used in a descriptive sense; for instance, an uncertain player is frequently told when his ball lies within fifty or sixty yards of the edge of a bunker, which he probably will not be able to carry, 'Just putt up to the bunker,' or he may be similarly advised when he has an approach to play, 'Just putt it up.' Such strokes are not putts within the real meaning of the word, but the expression well applies to the kind of stroke intended to be made, namely, one that will roll the ball up. In dealing with the subject, my remarks will apply only to putting in its strict sense.

Attention has already been directed to the necessity for playing approaches with accuracy; still greater, however, is the necessity for good putting. A stroke is defined as 'any movement of the club which is intended to strike the ball'; a drive of a couple of hundred yards and a putt of six inches equally count a stroke, notwithstanding the disparity of distance. It will easily be understood how a few badly played putts will make all the difference between a good and a bad score. Two strokes on each green may be regarded as the proper allowance for first-class play, three strokes means that one too many is taken; and if the latter number be required at each hole, it makes a difference of eighteen strokes on the round. It has before been stated, when treating of the subject of approaching, that a golfer who can lay the ball hear the hole with his approaches has a chance of saving a stroke on almost every putting-green against an opponent who does not play this part of the game so accurately, provided always that he can putt well; the proviso is most important. Unless the golfer is able to follow up with good putting the advantage gained by his approaches, the benefit is quite thrown away, and he is not in any better position than is his opponent who is less skilful in that particular part of the game. There is not a great number of holes on any links which require, bar hazards and mistakes, three strokes to reach the green from the tee; and leaving the difference to the score altogether out of account, it must be very humiliating to most players to know that they have required as many strokes to cover the last twenty yards of distance as it has taken them for the previous four or five hundred yards. Putting is therefore probably the most important part of the game, as no player who putts indifferently can ever hope to excel, however proficient he may be in driving and approaching. It thus behoves golfers to pay great attention to putting.

Putting has changed a good deal of recent years. Formerly the only club used was the wooden putter. In more modern times innovations in the shape of putting-cleeks and iron putters began to appear, and these have now to a large extent displaced the older implement. It is difficult to say whether the change is for the better or not. The upholders of the old wooden putter defend it with great zeal, and the believers in putting-cleeks are equally assertive of the merits of their club. Both are probably good in their way. For a long run up of thirty or forty yards or so, or even further – an approach putt, in fact – the wooden putter is still unequalled, and I also think that it is a good club to use where the putting-green is perfectly true and smooth. There is this disadvantage, however, that if the ball happens to lie in a nick it is apt to jump off a wooden putter. For the putting-cleek, it is claimed that it has all the advantages of the wooden putter, and that the ball can be kept under greater control when played off iron than off wood. I incline to believe that this is correct, and I have found that with a putting-cleek the ball can be hit harder in proportion to the length of the putt. On a rough green this is a distinct advantage, as, more strength being put into the stroke, the ball which will travel with greater speed and will pull up more quickly is less liable to be deflected by inequalities of the ground. My belief is, shortly, that for good, smooth greens the wooden putter is still able to hold its own, while for rougher greens a putting-cleek can be used to greater advantage. Taking all things into account, and if a golfer desires to use one club only for putting on all greens, I would recommend him to adopt a putting-cleek as likely to prove the more useful for all-round play. A putting-cleek is preferable to an iron putter, and should have a little loft on the face. Some players use an ordinary cleek for putting, but by doing so they put themselves to disadvantage. The flat lie of an ordinary cleek is against proper control being obtained over the ball, as it necessitates standing too far from it; the long shaft, too, is apt to catch and spoil the stroke, and on an ordinary all-round cleek there is usually rather more loft than is desirable for putting.

For putting, the grip of the club may, subject to the remarks made in Chapter III, be taken to be the same as that for driving and approaching, so far as the position of the hands is concerned. There is, however, the very important difference that the right hand should hold more firmly than the left, thus reversing the rule for the grip in other parts of the game. Putting should be almost all done with one hand, because, when both hands are used, the one acts against the other; the right hand is the hand which guides the club, and guiding the club is everything in putting, especially in short putts. With regard to the part of the club-shaft to be grasped, there is the greatest possible diversity of practice. Some players grip the putter just above the neck, and crouch down to play; others stand erect, and grip the club at the extreme end; and players may be seen with grips all over the shaft between these extremes. I do not think either extreme conduces to good play, and neither is graceful. The putter should be grasped on the leather at such a place as to give the player easy command of his club without contorting his body.

FIG. 38 – PUTTING – ADDRESSING THE BALL

The stance differs slightly from that for either driving or approaching. It is shown by the illustration, Fig. 38, and the diagram, Fig. 39. Here, as in the former case, *b* represents the place of the ball, and *aa* the line of play. It will be seen that the feet are placed much closer together, that the ball is nearer the right foot and also nearer the player, that the right foot is placed considerably in advance of the left, and that the knees are more bent. In this position, which is the one usually adopted, the weight of the body, while supported on both legs, is mainly borne by the right leg.

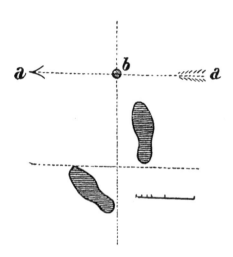

FIG. 39 – PUTTING – DIAGRAM OF POSITION

Off the left leg may now be regarded as a recognised position for putting. It is sometimes adopted by players who drive and approach off the right leg; and while I do not recommend that different styles should be cultivated by the same person for different parts of the game, varying the attitude does less harm in putting than in anything else. We constantly see the best players altering their stance from time to time, and putting equally well from all positions; in the short game there is the greatest scope for golfers humouring a passing fancy, pro-

FIG. 40 – PUTTING, OFF THE LEFT LEG – MR LAIDLAY
ADDRESSING THE BALL

vided a stiff and cramped attitude is not acquired. Mr Laidlay is again our authority, and an illustration (Fig. 40) and a diagram (Fig. 41) of his position are given. As in approaching, the body is thrown over to the left and the weight rested on that leg. A few years back Mr Laidlay's position was different, but always 'off the left leg.' He stood with the ball almost opposite the toe of his left foot, and placed the right foot behind the line of the left, and not in front as above shown. I may remark, however, that his putting has not suffered from the change; it is still of the same characteristic deadliness as formerly.

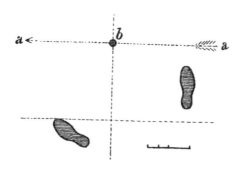

FIG. 41 – PUTTING – DIAGRAM OF MR LAIDLAY'S POSITION

There are two methods of putting in vogue: the one is putting for the hole itself, and the other is putting over a line to the hole. Holing a long putt is a matter of secondary consideration; the proper play is to endeavour to lay the ball near the hole – to 'lay it dead,' in golfing language – with the view of making certain of getting it down with the next stroke. This is subject to the remarks to be hereafter made. On the other hand, *all* short putts ought to be holed, and a *proportion*, varying according to their distance, of putts of average length ought also to be holed. For all putts the proper way is undoubtedly to play over a line to the hole. In explanation of this, it may be stated that, in the intervening ground between the hole and the ball, there must be a spot over which the ball will pass in its course to the hole. This spot, which shows the line to the hole, having been ascertained, all that is required to be done is to play over it with the requisite strength to reach the hole. It is not permissible (see Rule 33) to place any mark or to draw any line as a guide; but even on the smoothest and best kept greens it is always possible to notice a blade of grass, or something of this nature, which will serve as a guide. Such a mark should be selected comparatively near the ball, because if it be far away one may as well not have it, but play directly on the hole: it is intended as an aid. There need not be any hard and fast rule which the player must observe in taking the line to the hole; but it will be found that the best way is either to stand behind the ball and look over it towards the hole, or to stand at the other side of the hole and look over it towards the ball. I prefer the latter mode. Standing in this position, it will not be difficult, after some little experience, to see the imaginary line which the ball must trace on its road to the hole; and somewhere in this imaginary line, near the ball, a spot or mark such as I have spoken of before should be selected. Keeping the spot in view, the ball should be played over it with sufficient strength to reach the hole. Upon the strength may depend the proper line to the hole, as, if the putt is 'bolted,' the line will be straighter and more direct than if it is 'dribbled.'

There will of course be great diversity in the nature of the ground to be traversed in the putts, and allowance must always be made for any irregularity or obstruction which lies in the way. A slight cup in the green may turn the ball off, or a ridge may make it impossible to get the ball down. In some cases the green may be found to lie on an incline or slope, the putt requiring to be played across. In such cases the line of putt will not be straight – as on level ground – because when the ball is played forward it will at the same time roll down the slope; hence it is necessary to play up the slope a sufficient distance to counteract the falling off, or, in technical language, it is necessary to 'borrow.' The line will be a curve, the curve beginning at the ball and ending at the hole. Having selected the spot to be played over, and estimated the strength required to reach the hole, the face of the putter should be adjusted accordingly and the putt played. It is usual to rest the club in front of the ball for an instant just before playing, and it is now settled that doing so is not a contravention of Rule 34; the practice is, I think, a help to good putting. It is, however, very much a matter of taste and opinion. If the putt be difficult, or if it be an important one, it is worth while to take some trouble with it. It may be an advantage to study the line both from the hole to the ball and vice versa, so as to ensure accuracy. At the same time it must be remembered that the line from each point of view will not necessarily be the same, and both may be correct, as there may be, and very often is, more than one road to the hole. Where both views give the same line, there can be no difficulty; but where each shows a different line, the player must exercise his own judgment as to which he will take. As I have said before, I invariably adopt the line seen by looking from the hole to the ball.

Golfers who desire to play the short game steadily and accurately will never regret taking plenty of time to their putts. It is a grand mistake to play hurriedly. At the same time I do not counsel an undue amount of time being spent near the hole; there is a limit beyond which one should not go, and hanging over a putt is by no means to be recommended; but plenty of time and care should be bestowed upon seeing that the proper line is obtained, and in placing the putter in the proper position. After this has been done play at once. If unnecessary time be taken, the putt is apt to grow more and more formidable-looking every instant, and when once such a feeling grows over the player, he may bid farewell to the hope of holing. He must also remember that he is not the sole occupant of the links, and must have some consideration for the players who are following up behind.

The art of putting lies to a great extent in the player having confidence in himself. If he goes up to his ball in the full belief that he can and will hole his putt, he has a better chance of doing so than if he is troubled with doubts about this and that rough place his ball has to cross, and if his vision is obscured by the dread of a missed putt. If he dreads the putt, the longer he hangs over his ball the worse it will appear, and the less likely is he to hole it. One of the secrets of putting is to hit the ball, and the ball only – a sclaffy style of putting is fatal; and, with the object of making absolutely certain of avoiding it, rather aim to strike the globe just the least thing above the ground. The ball should be smartly tapped with the putter, the stroke being played entirely from the wrists; and it should neither be struck a slow, heavy blow, nor shoved, nor should it be jerked. Care should be taken to see that the putter is drawn straight back in the line of play, and brought forward in making the stroke in the same direction, so that only a forward movement is imparted to the ball; if this be not attended to, the ball may be sliced or pulled in exactly the same way as in the long game, and with similar effect, the result being that the ball will go past the hole instead of in. After having got the line of play and adjusted the head of the putter thereto, a final glance may be given over the line to the hole, just to make sure that everything is correct, and to gauge the requisite strength; but keep the eye on the ball when making the stroke. The face of the putter must not be inclined in, so as to hang over the ball.

It is not a good system of putting to dribble the ball into the hole. A putt should be boldly played, and the ball should strike the back of the hole and fall in; one constantly hears a player being coached to 'play for the back of the hole,' and it is one of the golden rules of golf, which has been handed down to us from former generations of players. When the putt is dribbled, there is no way on the ball, and the least inequality of the green will turn it off the line. There is another trite maxim for golfers, which has the like savour of antiquity, viz. 'Never up, never in'; unless there is some excellently good reason to the contrary, such as the state of the green on the other side of the hole, a putt should never under any circumstances be short. If the ball be not up to the hole, it cannot possibly go in. A well-played putt which misses the hole should be, in the case of putts of long or average distance, from a couple of feet to a foot past, and, in the case of short putts, about six inches past. Not being up is characteristic of a weak game, and, I think, helps to break down a player much more than does being too strong.

A putt down hill is somewhat difficult to negotiate, because it cannot be played boldly, but must be dribbled, and there being little pace on the ball, it is apt to be deflected off the line of play. These down-hill putts frequently require little more than that the ball be put in motion, and, gathering speed as it goes, the ball, if it misses the hole, will often roll out of holing distance for the next stroke. I prefer to play such putts with an ordinary cleek, as enabling back spin or bottom to be put on the ball, which helps to check its rolling too far. A little judgment and forethought will often obviate the necessity for having such a stroke to play. One should endeavour to avoid playing the ball into such a position that a down-hill putt will be the result, and should rather try to keep the ball at the low side of the slope, leaving a putt up hill, which can usually be boldly played with success.

FIG. 42 – A STYMIE

It is on the putting-green that there occurs the position of the balls known as a stymie, and which is shown by the illustration, Fig. 42. After being struck from the tee, the ball furthest from the hole must be played first, and a stymie is caused by the opponent's ball lying on the putting-green between the hole and the ball that has to be played. According to Rule 20, when the balls in play lie within six inches of each other, measured from their nearest points, the ball nearer the hole shall be lifted until the other is played, and shall then be replaced as nearly as possible in its original position. It will thus be seen that when a stymie has to be played, the balls must be at least six inches apart. There are two ways of playing stymies: the one is by using a putter or cleek, and putting on sufficient heel or pull to screw the ball which is being played round the opposing ball; this, however, is seldom successful, unless both balls are a few feet from the hole, and there is sufficient distance between them to permit of the heel or pull taking effect, or unless the nature of the green helps the ball to curl in to the hole. The other method – and it is the best one – is to loft the ball which is being played over the opposing ball. This stroke is best played with a lofter, or, in default of that club, an iron or mashie. The club must be grasped firmly, as for putting, and the ball struck sharply from the wrists, the strength being proportionate to the length of stroke. In stymies near the hole some players loft the ball right into the hole, while others prefer to make it loft on the green just short of the hole, and roll in. Both methods are equally good, if successful. Where the balls lie at the distance of a yard or so from it, it is hardly possible of course to loft the ball into the hole, and it must be lofted over the opposing ball and allowed to roll in. The stroke is by no means so difficult as it appears to be at first sight, and with a little practice one will be astonished to find how often he can negotiate a stymie successfully. The chief requisite is nerve. The taking out of a couple of balls and practising stymies is, however, quite a different matter from playing one in a match. The stroke is a very delicate one, and the least inaccuracy means a foozle, and the danger, which is great, of either missing the hole and running out of holing distance for the next stroke, or, worse than that, of hitting the opposing ball and knocking it into the hole. Even the best professional players will seldom play a stymie, unless they require to hole in that stroke to obtain a half. I would therefore say to every golfer who has been laid a stymie, and the opposing ball lies dead, if he has to play the odds, he must risk playing the stymie, because it is his only chance to halve the hole; but if he is playing the like, he is better to putt past the opposing ball with the view of laying his own dead, and so making absolutely certain of a half, than to risk playing the stymie, with the possibility, on the one hand, of being successful, and so gaining the hole, and the chance, on the other hand, of foozling and losing the hole – not getting even a half.

CHAPTER SEVEN

Play Out of Hazards

A GOLF-LINKS ENTIRELY devoid of hazards would be a very poor place indeed. Notwithstanding the amount of abuse lavished upon all hazards in general, it is to their presence that the game owes much of its interest. When I refer to hazards in this manner, I mean legitimate hazards judiciously placed; because a links, otherwise good in character, may be entirely spoiled as a first-class green owing to artificial hazards being formed, or to natural hazards being interposed, at improper places. The one object of the hazard ought to be that of punishing a badly played stroke, and in a subsequent chapter I shall deal more fully with this subject. There is no player so perfect but that at some time or other he is bound to get into difficulties. Among first-class players, he who gets into the fewest difficulties ought to be the best. The getting into a hazard ought not to seriously affect a golfer's chances of success in any competition, provided he does not repeat the mistake too frequently; and yet how many instances could be quoted of even a single error in this direction ruining a score which, till then, had left little to be desired! The punishment meted out in a hazard is twofold: in the first place, the golfer is penalised by the additional stroke or number of strokes required for extrication; and, in the second place, he is penalised by the moral effect it has upon his game; the latter is frequently by far the more severe punishment of the two. At nearly every competition we may hear golfers say, 'I played a good game till I got into that bunker.' This, translated into plain English, means that the moral effect of getting into the hazard was to break up the player. Upon a hardened golfer there should be no such effect. Before beginning the game, he must be well aware that he cannot hope to avoid every hazard;

but he ought also to know that any mistake he may make will not cost him more than one stroke, and he should never lose his head and allow his play to become loose on that account. It should have quite an opposite effect: he should rather endeavour to make up for his mistake by playing a more perfect game.

Hazards are defined in the rules of the game – Rule 15: 'A "hazard" shall be any bunker of whatever nature: water, sand, loose earth, molehills, paths, roads, or railways, whins, bushes, rushes, rabbit-scrapes, fences, ditches, or anything which is not the ordinary green of the course, except sand blown on to the grass by wind or sprinkled on grass for the preservation of the links, or snow or ice, or bare patches on the course.' This rule must be read in conjunction with Rule 14: 'When a ball lies in or touches a hazard, the club shall not touch the ground, nor shall anything be touched or moved before the player strikes at the ball, except that the player may place his feet firmly on the ground for the purpose of addressing the ball, under the penalty of the loss of the hole.' It will be seen that the last quoted rule prohibits the club being rested behind the ball, with the view of taking a good aim preparatory to the stroke being played. The object of this is pretty clear; it is intended to prevent the position of the ball in a hazard being improved. Take the example of a ball in a sand bunker. Here the ball, getting into the hazard, is practically certain to imbed itself more or less in the sand, and, if the club-head were rested behind, the sand would be pressed down, making the extrication of the ball comparatively an easy matter.

When a ball gets into a hazard, the one thing to be kept in view is to get it out. A great deal depends upon the position in which the ball is lying; sometimes it may be lying so badly that even to extricate it is a matter of considerable difficulty, while at other times it may be lying practically teed. Whatever the lie may be, the player should never allow himself to forget the primary object in view, and to be beguiled into attempting to try a difficult stroke with the view of making more of it. Such strokes usually fail, and leave the ball where it was before – in the hazard.

The most legitimate and ubiquitous hazards to be found on golf-links are sand bunkers. The sand in these is seldom smooth, but is generally pitted all over, more or less deeply, with footmarks of previous golfers walking through them, and into one of these footmarks the ball of the erring player usually finds its way. The best club to use, as before pointed out, is a niblick – failing that, a mashie. It may be considered somewhat absurd to speak of the stance and grip of the club when playing out of a bunker; but as some golfers may be troubled with doubts on this head, I have thought it well to say a word or two on the subject. Where it can be done, the position to be taken up should be the same as that indicated in the chapter on play through the green. The stance should, however, be taken up closer to the ball, and the club should be grasped on the leather firmly with both hands. A too short grip of the club takes away from the leverage afforded by the shaft; it is essential that a firm footing be obtained. It will not always be possible to take up the position desired, owing to the lie of the ball, which may be close to the side of the bunker, and in that case the player must suit himself to circumstances and stand as best he can. He may have to play with a foot in the bunker and a knee on the raised side of it. There is even said to be a case of a golfer playing with one foot placed on the back of his caddie. For the truth of this, however, I cannot vouch; but, in a recent match, the referee refused – and, I think, rightly – to permit of such a thing, which was suggested. Where the ball is not imbedded too deeply in the sand, and where there is no opposing side (or face, as it is generally termed) – as may be the case in a shallow bunker – the ball itself may be struck; but when it lies buried, or when there is a face over which the ball must be lofted, as will invariably be the case in a deep bunker, the sand behind the ball, and not the ball, must be struck, and the club-head dug deep into it. The force of the stroke is communicated to the ball through the sand, and results in its being baffed out. It is important to keep in mind that the further behind the ball the stroke is delivered, and the deeper the sand be dug into, the higher will the ball rise in the air, and the less distance forward will it travel. There is, of course, a limit of distance behind the ball within which such a stroke will have any effect, and the effect depends on the consistency of the sand; but if the sand be the ordinary dry sand to be found in bunkers on a seaside links, the hit should be made from an inch to a couple of inches behind the ball, depending upon the height of the face to be surmounted. The stroke should not be played with a sweep, but with an up and down motion; in fact, the head of the niblick should come almost straight down behind the ball. In these strokes out of bunkers every ounce of strength at the command of the player may usually be put into them without much risk of failure. A weak stroke in a bunker is useless, because the sand takes off so much force that the ball will probably not even be moved, and the more force, therefore, that can be exerted the better. I do not mean to encourage wild hitting, as accuracy is as desirable in this as in other parts of the game. It may be laid down as a hard and fast rule that a full stroke should always be played when the ball lies in a bunker, whether it is desired to drive the ball out as far as possible, or whether the bunker is close to the hole being played to. In the latter case, it may be that all that is needed to put the ball near the hole is to get it out of the bunker; nevertheless, I would still say, take a full stroke, and regulate the distance by the amount of sand taken – that is, if a long shot be desired, hit the ball, or as near the ball as is possible, and if it is desired merely to get the ball out, hit deeper into the sand a little further behind it. This is to be regarded as a general rule, and subject to obvious exceptions; for instance, if the ball be lying fairly clear, on smooth sand close to the putting-green, in such a case a carefully played wrist shot with an iron or mashie would probably give a better result than any other stroke.

I have already pointed out that a ball in a bunker may sometimes be found teed; such a ball is not to be lightly regarded. The safest course is generally to play it in the same way as any other bunkered ball, and to attempt nothing more than mere extrication from the hazard. Many players will, however, not be content with this, but will endeavour to make more of the stroke, and for their benefit I would make the following remarks. It is of course obvious that a club with sufficient loft must be used if there is a face to clear, and in that case a cleek or an iron will be the proper club to take, as circumstances may require. There may, however, be cases where the bunker is shallow and there is no opposing face – where the ball is, in fact, rather in a sandy lie than in a bunker – and then I consider that a brassy is the best club to use, if the ball be lying clear enough and if distance be required. I know some golfers think that a wooden club should never be used when the ball lies in sand, but with these gentlemen I cannot entirely agree, and for this reason: the sharp, narrow sole of an iron club tends to plough its way deeper and deeper into the sand if the ball be taken the least bit heavy, and thus the force of the stroke is lost before the ball is reached; whereas, when a brassy is used, the broad sole prevents, to some extent at least, the club from cutting into the sand, and helps to make it skiff over the surface. The aim must, in playing these teed balls, be accurate, and the ball swept away – as in driving – as cleanly as possible; it is surprising how much force will be taken out of the stroke if the club catches the sand ever so slightly.

A ball lying in water is the subject of special rules; but these rules do not derogate from the right to play the ball as it lies, if this be possible and preferable, in the option of the player. Rule 21 runs: 'If the ball lie or be lost in water, the player may drop a ball under the penalty of one stroke.' The method of dropping a ball is regulated by Rule 19, which states: 'When a ball is to be dropped, the player shall drop it. He shall front the hole, stand erect behind the hazard, keep the spot from which the ball was lifted (or, in the case of running water, the spot at which it entered) in a line between him and the hole, and drop the ball behind him from his head, standing as far behind the hazard as he may please.' It can hardly be supposed that any one will elect to play a ball out of water, unless it be out of a small, shallow pool, such as may have been caused by a shower of rain. Out of such a pool there is no reason why a good stroke should not be got, provided the player is willing to run the risk of a little splashing. There is, however, less danger of getting splashed than might be supposed, as the water will be thrown forward with the stroke, and very little will touch the player. I have no special advice to give on the subject of playing such a stroke, except that an iron club ought to be used, and the eyes must be kept open. The latter recommendation seems somewhat absurd; but there is an involuntary disposition to close the eyes as the club comes down, presumably to avoid the splashing.

Paths and roads are enumerated among hazards. If there be no stones to prevent it, the proper club to use for playing off these is a brassy. Get well down to the ball, and do not be afraid of hitting the ground. A club is much more liable to be broken through topping the ball than by sclaffing, even when the surface is hard.

A ball among stones is a very difficult one to play. Stones, in fact, are not a golfing hazard at all, and there should practically be no circumstances under which a ball can get into this position. In the majority of cases it will be unplayable. If, however, there is the possibility of extrication, a niblick or mashie should be used, and attention paid to the accuracy of the stroke.

After sand bunkers, whins are probably more frequently met with than any other hazard. Bushes, rushes, and hazards of this nature may all be classed together. There is a good deal of chance in the position in which a ball may be found in these; sometimes it may be unplayable, and at others a good stroke may be got. Everything depends upon the position of the ball. An iron club should almost invariably be used, and the general rule that extrication is the object to be attained should be kept in view. In rushes and long tufty grass a ball may sometimes be found lying teed on the top of a tuft. Like a teed ball in a bunker it is not to be trifled with. If the stroke be taken heavy, the club will cut right under the ball, and cause it to jump into the air without travelling any distance.

Take plenty time to the stroke, and hit the ball as accurately as possible. To these last-mentioned kind of strokes a brassy may sometimes be used.

The club should always be held firmly, to prevent the possibility of its being turned by catching an obstruction.

It is not always necessary to play a ball straight forward out of a hazard. This may at times be impossible; and it will frequently be more advisable either to play it forward in a slanting direction, or to play out to one or other side, or even to play back. The ball should be played as it will in the circumstances best go.

There is a good deal of scope for the exercise of individual ingenuity, and a golfer who keeps his wits about him may often make more of a ball in a difficulty than at first sight seems possible. But the elementary principles having been stated, he must deal with each contingency as it arises, according to his own judgment.

CHAPTER EIGHT

General Remarks on the Game

TO WRITE A CHAPTER of general remarks on the game might become a very serious undertaking were no limit placed upon the nature of the subject. This book is intended as a guide to golfers in playing, and hence the general observations I have to make will be strictly confined to what may be of service in this way, and to such matters as cannot be conveniently dealt with in any of the previous chapters – matters which apply to the game as a whole, and not to any specific part of it. The chapter will necessarily to some extent be disjointed, but this I cannot well avoid.

Accidents will happen to the best of players: clubs will break, and balls will be lost. What can be more annoying, or can handicap a golfer more severely in a match, than the breaking of his driver just after starting for the round, and the having to play the rest of the game without an efficient substitute? To provide against breakages and similar contingencies, it is well to carry a spare driver and brassy. In playing friendly matches, and in practice games, the breaking of a club is of less importance than in playing in a competition; and, in the former cases, one may choose rather to run the risk of breakage than to burden himself with extra clubs. The carrying of additional clubs is no doubt a consideration where caddies are not to be had; and, if he objects to this, he must weigh up the advantages and disadvantages in his own mind, and act accordingly. With regard to balls, it is a safe plan never to take out fewer than half a dozen. Not only is there the risk of losing one or two, or of them splitting or becoming unplayable, but it is a fact that the life of a ball is of very short duration. A few hard strokes, or a badly topped one, and the 'life' is out of the ball, after which it will neither drive nor putt so well as it ought to. Speaking for myself, I may say that, when playing an important match, I seldom or never use the same ball for more than four or five holes; and of course, if I happen to hack one in a bunker, I put down a fresh one at the first opportunity. I know many amateurs who follow this rule in playing in club competitions. The old balls do well enough for practice.

In golf there is a great deal in fancy. If one takes a dislike to a club, he will never play well with it while the dislike lasts; and, on the other hand, if he takes a fancy to any particular club, be it driver or brassy, he will probably play better with it than with any other club he can get, and will use it to good purpose for almost any kind of stroke. In such circumstances he cannot do better than humour his fancy.

Undoubtedly the best and speediest way to learn golf is to obtain the services of a professional who is willing to act as a 'coach,' or to ask the assistance of a brother golfer who has attained some proficiency. An experienced eye will point out faults and the remedies for them, which it might take a beginner a long time to discover for himself. There is no better method of acquiring a good, free style, than by practising swinging the club, a mark of some kind being placed on the spot which the ball should occupy in actual play. Even for golfers who have long passed the initial stages, there is no better exercise than this; it brings up and hardens the muscles, and will add some yards to the length of the drives. There is very little good to be derived by a beginner from playing rounds of the links until he is able to handle his clubs properly; he will derive much more benefit from practising the various strokes. After he has acquired the proper style of swing, he can take a few balls and go to an unfrequented part of the links, where he will interfere with no one and no one will interfere with him, and there practise drives, brassy shots, and iron strokes. He will attain proficiency much more rapidly in this than in any other way, because he will more readily see where he makes any mistake, and he can again at once play another stroke of the same nature, correcting his previous error; whereas, if he is playing a round of the links, the stroke he desires to perfect may occur only twice or three times. Of course, to practise putts, it is necessary to be on a putting-green; but opportunities for this can usually be obtained by choosing a day and hour when few players are on the links. There is no better mode of acquiring instruction than by watching the play of a good golfer. A great deal is to be learned from seeing a good match. After a beginner has got to the stage of knowing the game, he cannot expect to derive much good from anything but steady practice, and he must not be disheartened because he practises a long time before becoming perfect. The game will come to him all at once, more probably than by a slow process of improvement. Some day he will find he can play a much better game than he has hitherto done, and from this point onward improvement will be more rapid, until, by continued practice, he reaches a state of proficiency. He must not be disheartened because he sometimes goes off his game. Such a temporary lapse is common to all golfers.

It is of great advantage to be able to play straight, and to be able to play the ball to any place desired. The most famous golfers have been remarkable for this more than for long driving. Long driving is not within the reach of all; it requires physical strength – principally strength of wrist – but straightness and precision of play can be cultivated by any one with a good eye and hand, and conduce more to good golf than long driving.

Golf, like all other outdoor games, is affected to a very great extent by the weather; but it is possible to play during all seasons of the year and in all weathers, unless, indeed, the ground is deeply covered with snow. A slight covering of snow of an inch or so deep does not prevent devotees enjoying their game, red balls instead of white being used. I do not mean to say that the game is under such circumstances a test of skill, but it is then a healthy exercise if nothing more. The weather may be said to affect the game in two ways: firstly, indirectly, by changing the condition of the links; and secondly, directly, by interfering with the play. Upon the first head it may be remarked that, as will be obvious to every one, dry weather and sunshine make the ground hard, and the putting-greens exceedingly keen. Under these conditions the long game can be played to most advantage, as the ball will usually roll a considerable distance on the hard ground; but the advantage obtained thereby is more than counter balanced by the increased difficulty in playing the short game – approaching and putting. It is not easy to make approaches, especially pitched approaches, lie near the hole, and with keen, slippery greens putting becomes very uncertain. On the other hand, when the ground is soft or wet after rain, the balls fall almost dead off drives and long strokes – they practically run no distance; but this again is compensated in the short game – approaches can be boldly played with success, and putts can generally be run up to the hole with confidence. Upon the second head, heat and cold affect players differently, and so does wet; but the chief factor to be reckoned with is wind. Wind not only affects the player, but it also catches the ball. A big man fares worse in a windy day than one of less stature, because, in the former case, it gets a greater hold of his shoulders and interferes with his swing. On very stormy days some men have difficulty in keeping their feet during the swing. But on the ball the effect is most visible – in driving, in approaching, and in putting. Driving with the wind, it is of course possible to get longer strokes, while against the wind the distance is very considerably diminished; and in this latter case, if the ball is not truly struck, and if there is any slicing or pulling, the effects are much intensified. If the ball be accurately hit, wind, whether blowing against the line of play or across it, will deflect the flight to a comparatively trifling extent. With a cross wind blowing from the player's left a sliced ball will certainly be a long one, but its course will be nearly semicircular; and if allowance be not made for this, the ball may be found as far from the hole as is the tee from which it has just been played. Similarly with a wind blowing from the player's right with a pulled ball. With favouring winds experienced golfers occasionally heel or pull their drives intentionally, with the object of getting longer strokes. Before attempting to do anything of the kind in a match, it is as well to make sure that the advantage to be gained is worth the risk, and also to be tolerably certain that success will attend the effort, as the condition of a golfer who plays for a pull but happens to get on a slice or heel instead is not to be envied. Playing for either heel or pull is a dangerous habit, and not to be encouraged save under exceptional circumstances. When it is done, due allowance must be made for the deflected flight of the ball. This as regards driving, and these remarks apply, though in a lesser degree, to approaching. As regards putting, a putt with the wind will require only a gentle tap as compared with a similar putt against the wind; and if the wind blow across the putt, allowance must be made for the ball being blown off the direct line. In driving with the wind a spoon or lofted club may be used with advantage, so as to get the ball well up in the air, and secure the benefit of the wind drifting it along towards the end of the carry. But in driving against the wind the lower the ball can be kept the better. A deep-faced club with a stiff shaft is best for this. Some players prefer, when driving tee strokes against the wind, to play a hanging ball, and others stand more over the ball – that is to say, they keep it nearer their right foot. I think the latter device is good, but the former is too risky. As I have said in a previous chapter, a lower tee should be taken, and be sure to play with a good follow-through.

One sometimes hears it said of a successful golfer that he 'plays with his head as well as his hands,' and the meaning of this remark is too obvious to require explanation. There are many little arts in golf which may be studied, and the attention to which will contribute to improve play. I do not for a moment suggest that any unfair advantage should be taken, or that even doubtful expedients should be resorted to, though within the strict letter of the law; the arts I refer to are quite legitimate, and matter of everyday practice.

When a golfer finds himself pitted against a long and strong driver, I would say, Do not fear him unduly. It is no doubt somewhat terrifying and disheartening to be matched against such a player; but golf does not consist of long driving; there is no disgrace in being out-driven, and one may make up for deficiencies in the long game by more accurate approaching and putting, which, as I have stated before, tell more than any other parts of the game. One should not even be afraid to meet a stronger all-round player than himself. He should play his own game entirely irrespective of his opponent, and if he cannot avoid being beat he should make as good a show as lies in his power. This applies with particular force to play in competitions for score. It requires some modification, as is hereafter pointed out, when the game is by holes; and it may be proper to run risks to save the loss of a hole or of the match.

Even when a golfer plays against one who is admittedly and undeniably his inferior, he should beware of regarding the match too lightly. There is a good deal of luck in the game even on the best greens, and a match is not over till it is won. I could quote cases of players being eight holes up with nine holes to play, and yet losing the match all through a contemptuous regard for their opponents. Some golfers play with great determination and pluck, and it is possible to realise too late that, an inferior opponent, who has been held too 'cheap,' has by steady play made the match his own.

It is a mistake, generally speaking, to run risks that can be avoided, and on this principle it is better to avoid a hazard if nothing is to be gained by playing over it. Cautious play of this description is usually termed 'pawky,' and my experience of pawky players is that they are very dangerous opponents.

As before pointed out, a ball must not be teed in front of the marks laid down, nor on either side of these marks, nor more than two club's lengths behind them. Two club's lengths are, roughly, a couple of yards, and a couple of yards may mean all the difference between driving over a hazard and driving in. It is a mistake, therefore, to throw away distance by teeing further behind the marks than is necessary to secure a good tee. It may, however, be an advantage to get as far back as possible, as, for instance, at a short hole, where a full cleek shot would not reach the green, and a driver or brassy stroke would carry past the hole. In such cases it may be expedient to tee as far behind the marks as is allowed, and play with a brassy; but this is one of the cases in which a player must use his judgment.

I would again counsel golfers to remember that it is better to get a ball a few dozen yards nearer the hole, out of a difficult position, than to try too much and run the risk of a miserable foozle.

Rule 11 enacts: 'In playing through the green, all loose impediments within a club length of a ball, which is not lying in or touching a hazard, may be removed, but loose impediments which are more than a club length from the ball shall not be removed under the penalty of one stroke.' It is well to take advantage of the power to remove loose obstructions; even if they do not actually interfere with the stroke, they are apt to catch the player's eye, and distract his attention from the ball.

Whether playing against a stronger or a weaker opponent, I consider that it is always an advantage to have the honour or privilege of driving first. If the opponent is a longer driver, one is spared the temptation, which is difficult to resist, of pressing to avoid being out-driven. I may illustrate this by an example which fell under my own observation. A fairly good amateur golfer was playing against a professional, who allowed him a stroke at every other hole. The amateur got the first honour, and kept it for the first two holes. The professional won the third hole, and going to the fourth drove off first. He was a longer driver by some yards than the amateur, and the latter pressed to get away a long shot, with the result that he topped his ball. For the next five holes the professional held the honour, and at each of these five holes the amateur foozled his drive. I can attribute this to nothing else than pressing with the view of emulating the professional's driving, and indeed this was perfectly obvious to every onlooker. On the other hand, when the opponent is not a long driver, the moral effect of being out-driven may be such as to influence his play very considerably, as was the result in the case above instanced.

It is a curious fact that golfers very frequently drive into a hazard they are doing their utmost to avoid. When there is a small obstruction, such as a post or a whin bush, at all near the line of play, though not actually in it, I have seen balls hit it frequently, although the players were endeavouring to avoid it, and the chances were much against its being struck. The only reason I can adduce for this is that if the mind be concentrated upon an object, the hands, working in concert with it, unconsciously direct the ball towards that object. When, therefore, it is desired to avoid a hazard, I would recommend players not to think of avoiding the hazard; but to concentrate their attention on the intended line of play, and blot the hazard out of mind altogether.

I have before referred to the necessity for playing with confidence and decision, and this is a matter which cannot be too strongly impressed upon golfers. At the risk of being tedious to the reader, I reiterate the statement. If one allows himself to lapse into indecision over any stroke, and first selects his cleek and then thinks of his driver, and finally compromises the matter by using his brassy, he courts disaster. Let, him look carefully at the lie of his ball, judge the distance to the hole, and play without further ado. Golfers should always make a rule, too, of holing out every putt. Some comparatively simple-looking putts are deceptive; and if the habit is acquired of considering these as good as down, and not playing them, the effect of playing them and not holing a few in a competition, when every putt must be played out, has a tendency to demoralise most men.

To play golf one must know the rules of golf thoroughly, and conform thereto in every respect. There is only one game of golf, and that must be played according to the strict letter of the law, or else it is not golf. It may be a game of driving a ball round a golf-course, but it is not golf. Nothing surprises me more than the fact that a number of really good players do not know the rules; but this, I am sorry to say, is nevertheless the case. They no doubt know the principal rules; but put them into a tight corner, and ask is this or is that allowable, or what is the penalty for doing one thing or another, and they are entirely at sea. If there is one thing a golfer ought to know thoroughly, it is the rules of the game he plays. Some years ago the rules were contained in a couple of pages of print, embracing less than a score of laws, but nowadays they have increased considerably in number and complexity. My own opinion is that they are still far from perfect, and I should like to see a simpler and more explicit, and a more generally applicable, code introduced. However desirable this may be, we must meantime accept them as they stand, and act accordingly.

A golfer who desires to improve and perfect his game should always endeavour to play with an opponent who is just slightly superior to himself – one who can, generally speaking, beat him by a hole or by two holes in the round of eighteen. If he chooses an antagonist of heavier metal, he will have the feeling all through the game of playing against odds he cannot hope to cope with successfully, and this will tend to make him press, and will in time break up his game and demoralise him completely; whereas, if he plays with one just a little better than himself, though he is playing against odds, he will know that he cannot be beaten by much, and that he has a chance, and it may be a good chance, of holding his own, or even of coming in victorious, and he will further know that if he desires to do this he must not indulge in loose play. His game will therefore be kept in a healthy state of tension. He should never permit himself to play under the conviction that he must be beaten. It is an undeniable fact that if a golfer once gets a fixed idea into his head that a certain rival can beat him, he will always play a losing game against that rival, although there may be nothing to choose between them as regards golfing ability. I can quote the case of two well-known players, who were at the time among the best of their day, and who were, in the opinion of those competent to judge, equally good players. Yet the one was invariably successful in his matches against the other, simply because he had got into the habit of beating his rival, who had come to look on defeat as a matter of course. A match between a good and an inferior player may be equalised by the former allowing to the latter a handicap of so many holes, or so many strokes to be taken at certain holes; but this never makes so good a match as a level game with a player of equal skill with oneself.

Golf is a fickle game, and must be wooed to be won. No good can be got by forcing the game; and unless one feels fit and has a keen interest in the match, it is better not to play. It is no use going out and playing a round in a half-hearted, listless, indifferent way. Playing in this way is ruinous to good golf; and whenever one loses interest in the game, he is better to stop playing until he feels he can throw his mind and his heart into it. There is no greater mistake than playing till one becomes stale. Further, golf is a business-like game, and should be gone about in a brisk, business-like way. It is far better to play and walk round the links smartly and quickly than to creep round at a snail-like pace. Therefore choose a partner who will not keep you back by slow play. It is impossible to play good golf if you are thinking of something else all the time, and if you have any business worries, leave them behind when you go to the links.

'Foursomes' are not generally regarded as of the same serious character, so far as golf is concerned, as singles. In a single each has himself and himself only to depend upon; but in foursomes one is apt to trust either too much or too little to his partner; and besides, there is frequently a good deal of bantering carried on between the opponents, which is hardly conducive to good golf. Nevertheless a foursome makes a very enjoyable game if the sides are well chosen. It is not every golfer who will make a good partner in a foursome, and it is not always the best two players who will win. Much depends upon the ability of the partners to adapt themselves and their game to each other's play, and examples are not wanting of two first-class players being beaten by two of inferior calibre.

A three-ball match is, I consider, one of the best forms of golf, and only little inferior to a single. By a three-ball match I do not mean each party playing against the other two – playing his own ball, as the expression goes – but one, a good play-er, playing against the best ball of the other two somewhat inferior golfers. This form of the game is of great benefit to the single player, who pits himself against the other two, provided the odds are not too great. On most greens three-ball matches are not within the rules of the green, and can be passed by a two-ball match.

The subjects of match and medal play are deserving of some remarks.

In match play the opponents are face to face, and each sees what he requires to do to win or to halve each hole as the game progresses, and must regulate his play accordingly. I have before recommended every one to play his own game, no matter against whom he is opposed, and this is a general rule which may be with safety adhered to. But, like all other rules, it is subject to modification, especially in match play. The modifications which may be necessary can best be illustrated by examples. Let it be supposed that in playing to a hole the one player's ball lies well, while his adversary's has got into a hazard requiring a couple of strokes for extrication. Under such circumstances the chances are that the first-mentioned player will win the hole, provided he does not make some dreadful mistake, and he ought to play with caution, and run no risks of getting into difficulties, in order to make absolute-ly certain of gaining the hole. He should remember that he has two strokes in hand, and should be careful to utilise them with the object of making sure of the hole. To win the hole he requires to get down in only one stroke less than his opponent; and if the latter takes seven strokes, nothing is to be gained by attempting to hole out in four or five strokes. Now, on the other hand, let it be supposed that our player's ball has got into a difficulty costing him a stroke, and his opponent with the like lays his ball on the green. It is almost certain, bar mis-takes on the part of the opponent, or bar exceptional play on the part of our supposed golfer, that the latter will lose the hole, and he ought to run every risk, however great – be it a long carry, or a difficult approach, or a tricky putt – in order if possible to snatch a half out of the fire. To put the matter shortly, in match play a golfer's game must be governed by the state of the match at the time, and he must play to win holes or secure halves quite irrespective of the number of strokes taken to any individual hole, or to the score for the round. Every one wishes to win his matches, and the way to do this is to hang in to your opponent. In a close match it is the player who can hang in that wins; and when playing against a superior golfer, if you hang in to him he will possibly be disappointed to find that he is not winning so easily as he probably expected, and this disappointment may in the long-run cause him to 'crack.' It is good principle to try and have your opponent beat 'before the finish,' *i.e.* before the last hole is reached.

I have frequently heard comments made upon the scores taken in playing matches; but, in the general case, such comments are manifestly unjust to the players. If the scores are low, the play *must* have been good, because a good stroke game can never be a bad hole game; but the play may have been equally good, and possibly even more interesting and brilliant, if the scores are high, and therefore a good hole game *may* be a bad stroke game. A hole and hole game and a stroke game are entirely different forms of golf, and to my mind the former is by far the more interesting and sportsmanlike, because both players always know how the game stands, and they are face to face with the man they have to beat.

In competitions by strokes matters are entirely different: each player is playing against a whole field, any one of whom may return a better total, and any one of whom, however well he may start, may break down at a critical moment, or may spoil his card by one bad hole. Hence each should play his best game without regard to the rest of the field, and without either risking hazardous strokes or shirking difficulties. It may happen that a competitor playing late in the day may know what he has to do. He may learn that a good card has been returned, and that he has to do the remaining holes in a certain number of strokes to beat that card, and in this case it may be necessary to run risks with the object of saving strokes; but this is an exceptional case, and does not frequently occur. I can, however, quote instances of it. I remember a Championship at Musselburgh some years ago in which Bob Ferguson played, when, after holing out at the third last hole, he was told he must do the remaining two holes in six strokes to tie; and he proved equal to the occasion. Unfortunately Bob lost in playing off the tie, otherwise he would have been the only golfer who had won the cup four times successively. Later still, at the Autumn Meeting of the Royal and Ancient Golf Club, in September 1893, Mr F G Tait had early in the day returned a score of eighty, which was considered unassailable. Mr Mure Fergusson, playing after him, knew at the sixteenth hole that he must do the remaining two holes in nine to win, and ten to tie. Those familiar with the course at St Andrews are aware that the direct line to the seventeenth hole from the tee is over the corner of an enclosure called 'the station-master's garden,' but it requires a long shot to carry this hazard. If successfully carried, however, it gives an easier and shorter road to the hole, making it an almost certain five. The alternative line of play is wide of the enclosure; but this makes the hole more difficult. Mr Mure Fergusson risked the carry, and was successful in doing the hole in five, and the next in four, thus winning the medal. These examples will show what golfers must occasionally do. The necessity for such play can only arise when the exact state of the scores of the other competitors is known; and it must be amply evident that this cannot happen very frequently to any individual. In the majority of cases he will have to play to the end in ignorance of the other scores, save that of his partner, and he must therefore play his usual game without either trying to do too much, or using unnecessary caution. It has already been advised that in playing for score golfers should never risk doubtful hazards, but rather play to the side or play short. In this, as in other matters, judgment must be exercised. I do not counsel golfers to play short of hazards they habitually carry, merely because they are playing in a competition. By such tactics more strokes may be lost than saved. It is absurd to risk a doubtful carry, but it is equally absurd to play a too cautious game. When on this subject, I would again draw attention to the rule under which a ball may, in a stroke competition, be lifted out of a difficulty of any description, and teed behind the same under a penalty of two strokes. It is far better to do this at once than to lose several strokes in a hazard. Apart from the loss of strokes, playing out of a hazard, especially a bad lying ball in a sand bunker, is hard work, and most golfers will find that they require to reserve their strength to sustain them till the finish of the game. The motto I would give to the golfer who desires to come to the front in playing competitions is, 'Never mind a bad hole. Blot the remembrance out of your mind, and play as if your past game had been perfect.'

In order to play first-class golf it is necessary for the player to possess physical strength. I do not say great strength; but, although golf is a game of science and skill, and although a very good game can be played by persons not physically strong, it is scarcely possible for any one to become a first-class player who has not sufficient stamina and strength to back up his skill. All our best players, both amateur and professional, are men of good physique – muscular and wiry. The requisite skill can only be obtained through constant practice; and before any one can consider himself really fit to take part in an important competition with the prospect of winning, he should through practice have brought himself to such a state of perfection at the game, that he will be able almost intuitively to know what he is to do at each stroke. He ought not to require to pause at any stroke and ask himself what he should do, but ought to know this instinctively. Between a player in practice and a player out of practice there is an immense difference, especially in the short game. I will take putting as the example; but the same remarks apply to all – driving, approaching, and putting. A man out of practice must carefully consider the strength of his stroke and the line to the hole, while if in practice his eye instinctively guides his hand; and even if he goes up to his ball and hits it unconcernedly it is likely to be a better stroke than he could, with all precautions and care, play if out of practice.

The amount of practice requisite will vary with different players. Some men can play for a long time and get steadier and better as the days go on. Others will come to their top game more quickly, and after that are apt to grow stale. I believe in constant practice when it can be got. To begin with, a round, or eighteen holes, a day will be found quite sufficient; as time goes on this should be increased to a couple of rounds; but after reaching top form there is a danger in playing too much. A couple of rounds twice or thrice a week is quite enough to keep in practice. My reason for advocating the increase of play from one to two rounds a day is, that all the golfing fixtures of importance demand, at least, thirty-six holes play: the Open Championship now requires seventy-two holes to be played – thirty-six each day – and in the Amateur Championship, which is conducted on tournament principles by playing matches, there is never less than three days' play of thirty-six holes each day. Now, this continuous play is a severe strain on competitors, and, unless one accustoms himself to successive days of golfing, he will in all probability, however good a golfer he may be, find himself unequal to the task, and break down through sheer physical exhaustion when he is just beginning to enter the last and critical stages. During the competition it is advisable to save oneself as much as possible by avoiding all unnecessary fatigue.

I have already referred to physical strength, and physical strength cannot be supported without good fare. The man who can sit down and eat heartily is more likely to keep himself in good golfing condition than one who neglects such precautions. I have known a golfer who considered himself too strong to play good golf, and who was actually in the habit of starving himself for some days beforehand when he had a big match to play. Nothing can be more ridiculous than such an idea.

In training for a match, I think it is a mistake to change one's ordinary habits of living, provided they be regular. Any change, unless begun in good time before the day of play, and afterwards adhered to, seems to be more conducive to putting one off his game than getting him into form. At the same time, it does no harm to take a rest from playing the day before a match.

During the actual play of a match one should steadfastly decline to hold conversations with officious friends or other persons, or even, unless when necessary, with his opponent. One should direct his entire attention to the playing of the game, and not suffer it to be distracted by anything whatsoever. The game, and nothing but the game, should occupy the player's mind if he desires success to attend him. A judicious caddie is of great assistance; but in regard to caddies I have something to say later on.

It will frequently happen that preliminary practice must take place over a different green than that over which the competition is to be played. This, of course, cannot be helped; but it is usual to go to the green fixed on for the competition, and have some games there a week or so beforehand. All that should be necessary at this stage should be to get some knowledge of the links. One should, however, be careful how he goes about this. If he plays a few rounds badly, he may take a dislike to the links which he will find it hard to overcome, and which may ruin his prospects of success. The principal things to find out are the positions of the hazards, the 'distances,' the best lines to the holes, and the nature of the putting-greens. A better idea of these can be formed by taking out a club and a few balls and having some trial shots than by playing several rounds. A quiet walk round the course, and some observation of the play of the local cracks, will not do any harm, and a good deal may sometimes be learned from so doing.

There are few golfers who do not, at some time or other, get out of form. The chief causes of this are: (1) golfing oneself stale; and (2) indulging in a vicious style of play which may possibly have crept on unawares. As a cure for both, I would say, 'Take a rest.' It is the remedy for the first; and as for the second, when play is resumed the bad habit will probably have been forgotten; but whether or not, it will be well when making the fresh start to pay particular attention to style.

The next matter I have to deal with is that of caddies. As is to be expected, the best caddies are to be found at Musselburgh and St Andrews, the head-quarters of golf; but these are men with whom club-carrying is a business and a science. Reference to the rules will show how important a part in the game is held by the caddie. A golfer and his caddie are regarded as one. Here are quotations from some of the rules: 'A player or a player's caddie shall not press down or remove any irregularities of surface near the ball,' etc. (Rule 16). 'If the player's ball strike, or be stopped by himself or his partner, or either of their caddies or clubs,' etc. (Rule 24). 'If the player, when not making a stroke, or his partner, or either of their caddies, touch their side's ball,' etc. (Rule 25). 'A competitor may not receive advice from any one but his caddie' (Rule 10 for medal play). There are other references to caddies in the rules, all pointing in a similar direction. The fault of a caddie is visited on his employer, who is entitled to look to his caddie, and his caddie only, for advice and assistance. A careless or ignorant caddie may ruin a golfer's chances of success at any competition by breaking the rules, and may also put him off his game through sheer inattention to his duties. A good caddie ought to be a good player, or, at all events, have a thorough knowledge of the game and of the rules, and of his employer's play. A man who has spent his life carrying clubs has a wonderful aptitude for discovering the good and bad points of the game of any individual, and after carrying for him for a few rounds will know just about as much of that individual's game, and the way he is most likely to play a stroke successfully, as the player himself; and no one has a better eye for seeing what is wrong when his employer is off his game, or is more likely to recommend the proper cure. The man a golfer wants for a caddie is one who can advise him as the game progresses, and for this great tact and judgment are necessary. One golfer may use a brassy or driver where another would use a cleek, and both, using their respective clubs, may play perfect strokes. Now, a good caddie, who knows his business, would not, if his advice were asked, oppose the use of a wooden club, but would rather enjoin its use, even although he knew it was not the proper club to use; and the reason is that when once a golfer has made up his mind to use any particular club, he will, if he changes it for another, be troubled in his own mind as to which he should take, and the result will in all probability be a foozle. Watch a caddie who knows what he is about. After the drive has been played, his eye never leaves the ball until it is holed out. A lost ball, unless it be driven out of sight, is an impossibility. Put down a perfectly new ball, and if it has once been struck, although there may not be a mark on it visible to the casual observer, he will pick it out from among a dozen almost identical. Golf-balls are like faces, and your caddie knows the face of your ball at once. Playing a stroke through the green, or an approach, his eye takes in the situation at a glance, and without hesitation he knows the club that you can best use, and he is handling it, or has half taken it out of the bag, when you are considering what you will do. Your eye falls on it, and you immediately ask for it and play. At the end of the game he can tell over again every stroke you have played, and could go round the green and lay the ball down on almost the exact spot from which it had been played, in any of the fourscore or more strokes that you have taken. He can generally tell you the best road to the hole, and on the putting-green his line is invariably the correct one. He is always at your elbow when wanted, and yet never lets his presence be obtrusive. One who will answer these requirements is a desirable caddie; but I know caddies who do more than that. I have known them stand between a nervous player and well-meaning friends, whose anxiety to see him win would have put him off his game. One doesn't ask the player how he stands in a match, he asks his caddie; and there is no arithmetical problem in the way of counting holes or strokes, in singles or foursomes, or in three-ball or four-ball matches, that a good caddie cannot answer correctly in a moment. Bad caddies may be ranked in two classes, the one being those who know what ought to be done and do not do it, and the other being those who know nothing whatever about their duties. Of the first I may instance the case of the caddie who insists on his employer using the club of his choice, and pestering him with unasked advice, which of course is not taken; and, the inevitably bad stroke being played, reproaches him for not having done as he was bid. The last words are strong, but I cannot put it in any other way. Of the other class, the ordinary example is the boy who simply carries your clubs. He walks round the links with you, some-times not at all near you – a few hundred yards away – and he takes no manner of interest in the game. He never knows where your ball goes to; if you give him two or three to carry he is sure to lose one, if not more, in the course of the round, and, unless specially watched, he will leave the ball you are playing with in the bottom of the hole. He lags behind, and when you want a club you have to wait for five minutes, and shout yourself hoarse before he comes to you. He cares for nothing but the pence he hopes to receive at the end of the day. Club carriers of these classes – for I cannot call them caddies – are worse than none. I do not say all boys are alike. On the contrary, some of them make fairly good caddies. It is true that few of them can give you any assistance, but they will always be at hand and give you the club you ask for. If you are able get a good caddie, who will supply the requirements before indicated; if such an one is not to be had, get an intelligent boy, who will keep near you; and, if neither is available, carry your own clubs.

Fore-caddies are not, on most greens, usually employed save in important matches.

In the rules of golf there are a few paragraphs devoted to what is called the 'etiquette of golf.' These have for the first time appeared in the printed rules in this form. In the older rules some of them appeared among the laws of the game. They relate, however, only to an inconsiderable part of the courtesy that ought to accompany the play of the game. This is not a subject upon which I would wish to enlarge, and I would merely say that golfers should act towards each other and towards the non-golfing public in the same manner as they would desire to be themselves treated in similar circumstances, whatever they may be. The usual mode of warning persons – whether engaged in playing or not – that they are in the way of a stroke, is by shouting 'Fore,' which is supposed to be a contraction of 'Before.' The warning shout should be given before the stroke is played, and no stroke should ever be played if there is a danger of the ball hitting any one. Being struck with a strongly played golf-ball is no light matter, and serious results might follow. It sometimes happens, however, that a ball may, by heeling, or pulling, or otherwise, in its flight travel towards persons who are considered out of its way when the stroke is played. In such cases it is not always wise to shout 'Fore,' as, for instance, if the persons are walking out of the way, with their backs towards the player, the shout will in all probability cause them to stand still, or to turn in the player's direction, with the result that instead of their walking out of harm's way, and the ball falling short of them or hitting them on the back, it may strike one of them in the face. It may in such circumstances be more advisable not to shout, but to trust to Providence.

CHAPTER NINE

Competitions and Handicapping

IT IS USUAL FOR golf clubs to hold three or four prize meetings or competitions in the course of each year. These are frequently named after the seasons in which they take place – as the spring, summer, autumn, and winter meetings – and sometimes after the more important prizes competed for, as the medal meeting and the cup meeting. Such competitions may be for scratch prizes, in which case the actual game of each competitor is alone regarded; or they may be for handicap prizes, in which case allowances are made to the weaker players, to place them on equal terms with the stronger players of the club; or they may be for both scratch and handicap prizes. In one club I know of – and it is a model club, embracing many of the best amateur players in Scotland – the only prizes offered for competition are scratch prizes; there are no handicap prizes at all. But in almost all other clubs it is usual, in addition to there being at least one scratch prize, to give a certain number of handicap prizes. The object of this is to encourage golf, and to stimulate the exertions of players who could never hope to win the scratch awards. It is obvious that if only scratch prizes are to be played for, the contest resolves itself into one among the best players in the club, and among them alone, because the vast majority of members would not take part, knowing that their chances of success were very remote. On the other hand, when handicap prizes are presented, every member of the club, be he a good or a bad player, has an equal chance of gaining a prize. I would accordingly recommend clubs to adopt this system of combining scratch and handicap prizes. There should be at each meeting a scratch prize and three or four handicap prizes, and at two of the meetings the scratch prizes should be made the important events in the club's competitions. For example, there may be a scratch gold medal to be played for at the spring meeting, and a silver cup to be played for at the autumn meeting. Important trophies, such as gold medals and cups, do not, as a rule, become the property of the winners; the successful competitors hold them for a year, and get their names inscribed on them, receiving at the same time a small medal or charm to be retained as a memento of their victory. Some of the cups and medals belonging to the older golf clubs are of great value, not only on account of their intrinsic worth, but also on account of the associations connected with them. Handicap prizes usually consist of articles of an ornamental or useful nature, but not of great value, as they invariably pass into the absolute custody of the winners. There may, of course, be scratch prizes of the same nature as the handicap prizes above mentioned, and which, like them, become the property of the winner; and, on the other hand, there may be handicap medals and cups, tenable by the successful competitor for a year only. The conditions under which the prizes are to be won may be varied to almost any extent. For instance, a prize, either scratch or handicap, may be given for the best aggregate score at any two, or at two stated competitions in the year; or a prize may be presented for competition to become the property of the player gaining it three times, or three times successively. Some clubs have a monthly medal or cup, to be held for a year by the golfer winning it the greatest number of times during the year, he receiving a charm or small medal as a memento. There is, however, this objection to such monthly competitions, that they interfere considerably with the private match play of the members of the club, and on that account they are frequently objected to. Such competitions are usually fixed for a day that will enable the greatest number of players to compete; and as it is the invariable rule, especially with clubs having private greens, that all competitions shall take the precedence of private matches, the day becomes practically devoted to the competition, thus debarring all play except in it, and this is considered to be more or less a hardship upon those golfers who prefer a friendly game. All players are in the general case allowed to compete not only for scratch awards, but also for handicap prizes, and it may thus happen that one man may carry off more than one prize; he may, for example, win a scratch and also a handicap prize. The stated competitions of all clubs are invariably played for under medal rules, or according to score. In addition to such meetings, many clubs hold an annual tournament, played during the summer months by holes, or under match rules. This is always under handicap, and in a new club is extremely useful in introducing the members to each other. In the first chapter I have referred generally to playing medal competitions and tournaments. There is not much to be added in regard to the former. The players start in couples, and it is for the management of the club to determine whether the players may arrange their own partners, or whether they are to be balloted for. If competitors are allowed to arrange their own partners, there is this advantage, that they may be allowed to start at any time on coming forward between certain hours; while, in the other case, the players must come forward in batches and be balloted for partners before they can start, thus entailing some congestion of the green at the hours of start. Where there is a ballot for partners, the order of starting is usually determined by the ballot – that is to say, the first couple drawn start first from the tee, and so on; but the captain of the club, if present, and his partner are always by courtesy permitted to go off before all others. Where the couples are balloted for, it is a good plan to divide the players into classes before the ballot takes place, because it is unfair to both if a good and a bad player be drawn together. I would recommend that all members having a handicap of less than, say, ten strokes, should be balloted for partners among themselves, those having a handicap of ten strokes and upwards being similarly dealt with. In handicap competitions under medal rules the scores for the prize list are reckoned by deducting the handicap of each player from his actual score, and the net result is his return in the competition. As is hereafter mentioned, some members of the club may, owing to their proficiency at golf, have a plus handicap, and this is added to the actual scores of such members. The following example of a prize list will explain the matter more clearly:

Name of Player	Actual Score	Handicap	Net Result	
A	90	- 8	82	First prize
B	83	- 0	83	Tie for 2nd and 3rd
C	78	+ 5	83	h'cap prizes. Scratch prize.
D	101	- 17	84	Fourth prize
E	87	- 2	85	

With regard to the conducting of golf tournaments, I may make a few remarks. It is usual to intimate that such a tournament is to be held, and to request intending competitors to send in their names within a limited time. Very often a small entry-money is imposed with the view of ensuring that only those who intend to play will enter, and in that case the entry-money is available for increasing the prize fund of the tournament. After their names have been handed in, the entrants are drawn against each other in couples. It will seldom happen that the number of couples will be exactly the number – such as 64, 32, 16, or 8 – which will ultimately reduce to 4, 2 and 1, and if not, it is necessary to draw a number of byes in the first stage, as byes in the later stages of the game are considered unfair. The number of byes being fixed, it is best not to have a separate draw for them, but to give byes to the couples first drawn to the requisite number. If this be done, all the couples obtaining byes must enter the play in the second round; whereas, if there is first a draw for couples and then a draw for byes afterwards, and if there be an odd man, he may draw a bye, and, having no opponent for the second round, will not require to play till the third round of the tournament. To determine the number of byes required, subtract from the nearest higher number (such as 64, 32, 16, or 8) which will ultimately reduce to 4, 2, and 1, the number of couples competing, and the remainder will be the number of byes. Subtracting this remainder (or number of byes) from the number of couples competing will give the number of couples who must play in the first round. I give two examples of how this works out:

First, suppose there are 49 entrants, that is, equal to 25 couples – because an odd man must in this case be regarded as a couple –

From the nearest higher number divisible as		
before, viz.		32
Subtract the number of couples,		25
	Giving	7 byes

which, subtracted from the number of couples entered, leaves 18 couples who compete in the first round.

Second, suppose there are 34 players, or 17 couples –

From the higher number as before, viz.		32
Subtract the number of couples,		17
	Giving	15 byes

which, subtracted from the number of couples entered, leaves 2 couples who compete in the first round.

In example number one the first seven couples drawn would receive byes, and the remaining eighteen couples would play in the first round, reducing their number to nine. These nine couples and the seven couples who drew byes, making sixteen couples, would compete in the second round, and thereafter, as before explained in the first chapter, the winner of couple number one would play against the winner of couple number two, and so on until the ultimate survivor was eliminated, who would be the winner of the tournament. The following table shows the method of arranging the draw: the first supposed example of there being forty-nine entrants has been adopted; each number represents the name of a player, and it is supposed that the first player of each couple always wins his match.

1st Round	2nd Round	3rd Round	4th Round	5th Round	6th Round

Byes

```
              1 }
              2 }  –    1 }
              3 }       3 }  –   1
              4 }  –             } –  1
              5 }       5 }
              6 }  –    5 }  –   5
              7 }       7 }                } – 1
              8 }  –                       }
              9 }       9 }
             10 }  –    9 }  –   9
             11 }      11 }                } – 9
             12 }  –                       }
             13 }      13 }
             14 }  –   15 }  –  12
   15 }      15 }
   16 }  –   15 }  –  15
   17 }      17 }     19 }  –  19
   18 }  –            23 }
   19 }      19 }                } – 19
   20 }  –   19 }  –
   21 }      21 }
   22 }  –
   23 }      23 }
   24 }  –   23 }  –  27
   25 }      25 }                } – 27
   26 }  –            27 }
   27 }      27 }     31 }  –  19
   28 }  –   27 }  –
   29 }      29 }                        } – 1
   30 }  –
   31 }      31 }
   32 }  –   31 }  –  35
   33 }      33 }                } – 35
   34 }  –            39 }
   35 }      35 }     35 }  –  35
   36 }  –   35 }  –
   37 }      37 }
   38 }  –                       } – 35
   39 }      39 }
   40 }  –   39 }  –  43
   41 }      41 }                } – 43
   42 }  –            43 }
   43 }      43 }     47 }  –  43
   44 }  –   43 }  –
   45 }      45 }
   46 }  –
   47 }      47 }
   48 }  –   49 }  –
   49   Bye
```

It will be seen that the winner of each couple is always carried forward another stage. In this case, if there were four prizes, No. 1 would be winner of the first prize, No. 19 winner of the second prize, and Nos. 9 and 35 would play for the third and fourth prize.

Having explained the competitions usually held by clubs, and the method of managing them, I will now deal with the question of handicapping. Handicapping in a newly formed club is a matter of vast difficulty, and it is impossible that all handicaps can be properly adjusted until the members have several times competed, and shown their exact form; and even then there are bound to crop up occasional cases of members with too generous handicaps, who carry off the honours of the meeting. This is unavoidable; because, however carefully the handicaps are adjusted, some players, especially young players, will improve so rapidly as to defy all attempts to handicap them accurately. Others, again, after playing a consistently bad game in former competitions, justifying their obtaining large handicaps, will come away with an occasional strong game very much above their usual average form. These are events over which the committee, to whom the handicapping is intrusted, have no control, and must be submitted to.

Handicapping may be treated from two points of view: first, as regards club meetings and competitions; and, second, as regards private matches. I will take them in this order.

As regards club competitions, there are two standpoints from which all handicaps may be adjusted. They may be adjusted with reference to the best or scratch player of the club, or with reference to a par or scratch score for the course. In the former case the handicap committee proceed in this way: they say A, the scratch player of the club, can give B six strokes on the round of eighteen holes, therefore we will give to B a handicap of six strokes, A playing from scratch. Under the other method they say eighty, or whatever other number they think fit, is par play for the links. A can go round in that score, therefore we will make him scratch; B takes eighty-six, therefore we will give to him a handicap of six strokes – and they deal in like manner with every member of the club. It seems to me that of the two methods the latter is preferable, because the par play of a links is always the same, while any player's form is liable to vary. It used formerly to be, and is still, in the old established clubs, a rule that no player, however indifferent his game, should receive a larger handicap than eighteen strokes, or a stroke a hole, the reason being that it was considered if he could not win with such a handicap, he did not deserve to win till his play improved; and it was thought that this had the effect of making the weaker players of the club desirous of improving their play so as to get within reach of the prize list. But in more modern clubs larger handicaps up to thirty or even forty strokes are allowed, every man being, in fact, handicapped on his form, whatever it may be. There is no doubt that this has the effect of inducing a larger turn-out of competitors, as frequently the more indifferent players are very enthusiastic devotees of the game. It should be kept in view that it is always better to give a player too small a handicap than too large, and no player should be handicapped until he has played at least once in a club competition. A record of all returns at competitions should be kept, and each member should be handicapped upon the average of his three best returns. Any player winning a prize should at once have his handicap reduced, the reduction depending upon the place he has attained in the prize list. Such a system of reducing the handicaps of prize-winners has been condemned, but in my opinion it is a good one, and helps to make the honours pass round. When a scratch player attains, as many do, such pre-eminence in his club that he is able to carry off not only the scratch awards, but also the handicap prizes, it is usual, rather than increase the handicaps all round, to make such a player plus so many strokes – that is, in fixing his handicap score so many strokes are added to his actual score instead of being deducted, as is usually done, and this works out easily and simply.

What has been written deals with medal play, or play for score; but club members require to be handicapped for tournament or hole play as well. The old practice was simple, viz. to give every player half as many holes as he had strokes; thus a player plus six strokes would be handicapped in a tournament plus three holes – that is to say, he would have to concede three holes to a scratch player; or, in other words, when he and a scratch player met in a tournament, the latter would start three holes up. Similarly a player with a minus handicap of twelve strokes would receive six holes of start, or six holes of a handicap. This has been found to work out fairly well, unless in exceptional cases; but it will readily be seen that it is not applicable to a club where members have thirty or forty strokes of a handicap; because, according to this practice, a player having forty of a handicap would start twenty holes up in eighteen against a scratch player, which is absurd. It is difficult to suggest a system of handicapping by holes for a club which gives its members large stroke handicaps; and under such circumstances the handicapping committee must take all the elements into account, and fix for each member a fair handicap by holes, apart altogether from his stroke handicap. Between stroke and hole handicaps there is this difference, that in medal play, if a golfer has one bad hole in the round, it may spoil his score completely, and ruin his chances of success, as its total must go into his card; whereas, in a tournament, a bad hole, however many strokes may be taken, means only the loss of one hole, and the golfer may retrieve his position by good play and winning the next hole. The majority of men who take big scores do not do so by consistently bad play, but by what may be called fairly good play coupled with two or three bad holes where they get into difficulties. A score in medal play is therefore not always a safe criterion from which to judge of a player's form in a hole game.

There is only one way of dealing with handicaps in medal play – that is, as before pointed out, by adding the handicap to the actual score in the case of plus men, and by deducting it in the case of men who have the usual or minus handicap. It is different in a hole and hole tournament. In the latter case the players may either receive a handicap of so many holes of start, as is before mentioned, or they may receive a handicap of so many strokes to be taken at certain holes. I do not, I think, require to say anything further about the case of giving a handicap by holes of start; but the giving of a certain number of strokes of handicap to be taken at definite holes requires some explanation. In this case the number of strokes to be given may, except in the cases of large handicaps, be the same number as that given for medal play, and the strokes should be taken at fixed holes; it is for those in charge of the tournament to arrange this. The tables annexed to the St Andrews Rules and to the Wimbledon Rules (printed in Chapter XI) may be adopted if either is considered suitable. That is to say, if a man receives eighteen strokes of a handicap from a scratch player he should take one stroke at each hole; if he receives six strokes, he should take one at every third hole, beginning with the second hole. Under this method, where two players are drawn against each other, one of whom receives a larger handicap than the other, the smaller handicap is deducted from the greater, and the player with the greater handicap receives from the other a handicap of the difference in strokes. Thus, if one player has a handicap of twelve strokes, and his opponent a handicap of six strokes, the former would receive from the latter the difference between their handicaps, viz. six strokes, to be taken according to the table. The tables are framed with reference to the links to which they relate, and the committee of another club may think that, owing to the nature of their green, neither is suitable for their club, in which case they must compile a table for themselves in accordance with local requirements. I have known competitions in which it was made a hard and fast rule that the strokes should be taken consecutively at the first holes – that is, if six strokes, at the first six holes, and so on; but I do not consider this is so satisfactory as having a proper table. With regard to the merits of the two methods of handicapping for hole play, I must say that my preference lies with the giving of strokes at certain holes rather than with the giving of so many holes of start, and for two reasons: in the first place, it more closely follows the usual system adopted in private matches; and, in the second place, strokes at certain holes are of more advantage to the receiver of the handicap than a proportionate number of holes of start. Take the case of a scratch player being drawn against one to whom he would have to allow, say, eighteen strokes in a medal competition, and suppose that the handicap of this latter player were for a hole tournament either nine holes, or one stroke at eighteen holes: in all probability the scratch man would take nine holes straight away off his opponent, thus having the match at his mercy; while, in the case of his giving a stroke at each hole, it would be very extraordinary if the stroke did not enable the weaker player to halve and to win several holes in the course of the game.

A table of match play odds, adopted by the Royal Wimbledon Golf Club, is printed at the end of the Wimbledon Rules, and may be found useful.

The method of playing 'Bogey' competitions has already been explained in the first chapter.

The handicap which one player should give to another in private matches is a matter of arrangement between the players, and may be adjusted as they please. It is purely a matter of bargain, and if two golfers play much together it will very soon work itself right. The usual way is for the one to give to the other the handicap of a stroke at certain holes; but there is no reason why holes of start should not be given if this system be preferred. An innovation in such handicaps is the giving of 'bisques' – that is, strokes to be taken at the will of the party receiving them. This is a very heavy handicap, and practically means that each bisque represents a hole, because, until the receiver has taken his bisques, they are always hanging over his adversary's head, and he of course takes them at such holes as are the most advantageous for himself. It may thus happen that a hole is halved in actual play, and that the receiver of the odds will then say to his opponent, 'I will take a bisque here, which makes the hole mine.' Similarly he may take a bisque so as to halve a hole which his adversary had otherwise won.

CHAPTER TEN

Laying Out and Keeping Golf-links

UNTIL A FEW YEARS ago a golf-links at a distance from the seashore was a thing seldom seen. True it is that there were one or two inland courses on which the game has been played for centuries, such as Bruntsfield, Perth, and Blackheath; but at almost every other place the sea-breezes and the music of the waves refreshed and soothed the jaded golfer, who obtained renewed vigour from a friendly match, unpursued by thoughts of his score or dreams of that demon of modern links, Colonel Bogey. As the demand for golfing facilities increased, it was impossible that the old courses could accommodate the numberless enthusiasts who threw themselves heart and soul into the game, and as a natural consequence golf-links have come to be laid out everywhere, very often on places which the past generation of golfers would have deemed it little short of madness to attempt to transform into a links. It has, in fact, been found possible to lay out a golf-course over almost any tract of ground of sufficient extent. The adaptability of the game is one of the greatest features of golf, and there are really few places where a course cannot be laid out. I do not say that a first-class links can be made everywhere that golf can be played, but a course can always be laid out over which many enjoyable games can be got, and on which a considerable amount of skill can be attained.

As is before pointed out, eighteen holes is recognised as the greatest number a golf-links should contain; and while it is desirable to have this number of holes, if good ones can be obtained, it is a mistake to cram into any piece of ground a greater number than it can comfortably hold. It is better to have nine good holes than eighteen bad ones.

The laying out of a golf-course is by no means a simple

task. Great skill and judgment, and a thorough acquaintance with the game are absolutely necessary to determine the best positions for the respective holes and teeing-grounds, and the situation of the hazards. It is a mistake to suppose that our older golf-courses in their present state are the same as when first formed. The original formation of them is lost in past centuries; but we know that changes have frequently been made, and they really have been the product of ages of experience, and have, so to speak, been evolved in the course of time. At every one of our historic courses changes have been made again and again as experience dictated – bunkers have been filled up and new ones formed, holes have been shortened and lengthened, until these links have assumed their present state.

When a new course is to be laid out I would strongly advise the promoters to obtain the assistance of some one experienced in such matters. But for the benefit of those who may desire to dispense with such assistance, or who cannot readily obtain it, I shall endeavour in this chapter to give an idea of the chief objects to be kept in view. It is not possible for any one who has not had previous experience of the game, and who has not seen other courses, to attempt to lay out a links. When, however, a new golf club is being formed, and a links being laid down, there is usually among the initiators of the movement at least one who has a good knowledge of the game, and such individual or individuals will usually take a leading part.

The most suitable ground for a links is undoubtedly that near the seashore; it will be found that however unpromising such ground may look at the moment, owing to a heavy covering of rough, benty grass, it will very soon improve with walking and playing over it, the rough grass will disappear, and a velvety sward take its place. A subsoil of sand is always in favour of ground being suitable. Ground at the seashore is not, of course, always available, and in default of it, any old pasture or moorland will usually be capable of being formed into a golf-links. I have seen fields of arable land sown down with fine lawn seeds to make an addition to an existing course;

but land so sown is the most expensive, it takes longer to bring into good condition, and is never so satisfactory in the end as land that has been under grass for some years. Sowing down land means making and turfing putting-greens, and it is not possible to get a good firm sole of grass before the second season at soonest. It should therefore only be adopted as a last resource.

The ground for the links having been selected, there cannot be much difficulty in ascertaining the number of holes it will contain. If there be sufficient space for eighteen good holes so much the better; but if not, I would recommend that the number be fixed at either nine or six, as twice round the one and three times round the other completes a game. Fifteen- and twelve-hole courses are sometimes found; but in either case the number is awkward, entailing the play over again of the first three or six holes, as the case may be, to complete the game, and it may happen that these first holes are by no means the best on the course, and, moreover, it may have the effect of terminating the game at a considerable distance from the club-house.

The number of holes having been decided upon, the next thing to settle is their position, and the position of the teeing-grounds. It is desirable that the first teeing-ground and the last putting-green should be near the club-house, so that members may neither have far to walk to begin their game, nor far to walk after it is finished. These two preliminary points settled, a bird's-eye view of the ground from some eminence may probably suggest the positions for the other holes and teeing-grounds. Having tentatively fixed the places for them, and found that they will all fit in in due order, the place of each should be marked off by a stake, and each hole critically examined in detail. If ultimately found suitable after due consideration, the places so indicated can be finally adopted. I need hardly say that a very great deal will depend upon the natural character of the ground; and although the following remarks are intended to guide in laying out the green, it will be found that in many cases they cannot be strictly adhered to, but must be varied to suit the nature of the ground upon which the links are being formed. It may be taken as a general indication of the length and difficulty of a green of eighteen holes, that par play over it – that is to say, good play without mistakes, and allowing two strokes for holing-out in each case after the putting-green is reached – should require about eighty strokes. I do not think it is advisable that any green should be more difficult.

In regard to the shape of a links, I personally think those on which the holes go straight out to the ninth and return in the opposite direction are preferable; but this must be decided by the nature of the ground, and the holes may be put down in any form or shape that is found most convenient. If possible, avoid making the line of play to one hole cross the line of play to another, and avoid the line of play to or from holes parallel to each other being too close. On a busy green crossing and playing in close parallel lines is apt to result in some of the players being struck; and even if accidents do not happen, timid players are kept in a state of constant trepidation.

The first two or three holes should, if possible, be fairly long ones, and should be, comparatively speaking, easy of play. Holes of a good length permit the players to get away without congesting the links, or, in the words of a Musselburgh caddie, it allows them to 'get squandered.' If the first holes are too short or too long or too difficult – any extreme produces the same result – there is invariably a block at the tees; whereas, if the plan I have suggested can be carried out, this is avoided. Another reason for having the first two or three holes comparatively easy is, that I consider it is only fair to permit a golfer to get warmed to his game before severely testing his abilities. A good start is all-essential, and even the best of golfers may get into difficulties. If he does get into difficulties at the first couple of holes it will materially affect his whole game and deteriorate his play; whereas, if he gets a good start, he is not only less likely to break down under the strain of difficult golf, but even if he does come to grief it will not have the same depressing effect on his after play. The green should be laid out so as to test the capabilities of golfers without giving undue advantage either to the man who is a long driver, or to the man who excels at the short game. A golfer who can drive further than his neighbours is undoubtedly entitled to some advantage for being able to do this; but, as golf does not consist solely of long driving, the advantage should not be so great as to put out of court entirely the man who, driving a shorter ball, is more expert in approaching and putting. There should, therefore, be a certain proportion of holes at each of which the long driver, by reason of his long driving, can save a stroke; and there should also be a certain proportion of holes at which the player who can handle his iron and his putter skilfully has a like advantage. On every eighteen-hole course there should be at least two short holes within the reach of a good player with one stroke; these should be certain three's. I would almost advocate their being in the one case a full cleek shot, and in the other a full iron shot; and there should be not less than one long hole to be reached in, say, three full strokes. The other holes may be made of varying lengths – none of them under two strokes in length, some capable of being reached in two full shots, and others within reach of one full drive or two full drives and iron and cleek shots of varying lengths. Holes which can be reached with a drive and an iron shot should, unless properly guarded by hazards, be very sparingly laid down, because they are likely to prove what has not inaptly been termed 'levellers' – that is to say, the ball can be driven on to the green in two strokes by anybody, and it may be that at such holes, if not guarded, there is little advantage in getting away a good drive, because, even if the drive is foozled, any ordinary player can put his ball on the putting-green with his second stroke. The result is, that one man who has driven a good shot may have a short approach to play, while another who has got a bad drive, or who has foozled his stroke, will only have a longer approach to play, and his mistake will thus cost him very little. Of course in this case there is an advantage in having to play the shorter approach; but, generally speaking, a mistake ought to pay a greater penalty than merely increased length of approach. If there be judiciously placed hazards, such an objection cannot hold good, as a foozled drive is practically certain to be punished. It is not possible to lay down ideal distances, because so much depends upon the nature of the ground. For instance, on a flat or on a seaside links, where the ground is hard and the turf short, a ball can be driven much further than on a hilly or heavy course, because it has a considerable run after alighting, and it is possible to get away a long second stroke owing to the ball lying clear; while on a heavy inland course, where the grass is long, the drive is all carry without any run, and owing to the interference of the grass it is not possible to get away a long second stroke; and on a hilly course, the nature of the ground may considerably diminish the distance of the drive; consequently, on courses of the nature first mentioned the holes may be made longer than on courses such as those last indicated. It is to be kept in view, too, that the links are to be laid out for the use of a certain class of golfers. If all are beginners it is a mistake to make the course too difficult at first, as it will diminish their pleasure and possibly disgust them with the green; but as they get more expert the links can be made more difficult by lengthening the holes and similar devices. On new greens which are of a rough nature, the holes should be made shorter to begin with, until the ground is walked down, and they can afterwards be lengthened by putting the tees further back; for, of course, the putting-greens cannot be removed save at great expense.

The tees should be placed on level parts of the course, with, if anything, a slight slope upwards in the direction to be played. If there be a hillock or rising ground or any obstruction requiring to be driven over in front, the teeing-ground should be kept far enough back to enable the ball to rise over it in the course of its flight. Provision should be made for changing the teeing-grounds frequently, to prevent the turf on them being worn out, and to permit ground previously used to recover.

The selection of putting-greens is a much more difficult

matter. The variety of places on which they can be formed is infinite. They may be on the level course, or in a natural hollow or basin, provided it be sufficiently large and shallow, or they may be placed on the tops of large 'tables.' All of these are good positions, and the more variety that can be introduced the better. The putting-greens should be as large as possible; and while the ground should be comparatively level, it is not desirable that it should be perfectly flat like a billiard-table, but should rather be of a slightly undulating character. It is absolutely essential that a putting-green be firm and smooth, and the turf close and short, so that the ball will roll on it and not 'bobble' or jump, as it certainly will if the turf be brushy and uneven. If natural putting-greens cannot be made on the course as it stands, then they must be dug up and laid with suitable turf; but this should only be done as a last resource. It is a very bad piece of ground that will not improve sufficiently to make a fairly good putting-green, under proper care, and with due cutting and rolling and top-dressing. A strong attempt should always be made to bring the natural turf into condition before resorting to the lifting and turfing of a putting-green. Many will be surprised to find the improvement that can be effected on any, ordinary turf with proper treatment and care. If large enough putting-greens cannot be made at any particular parts of the course, it may be necessary to have relief putting-greens on to which the hole can be changed when the regular greens show signs of tear and wear. The putting-greens and teeing-grounds should, as previously pointed out, be in proximity to one another.

With regard to hazards, I would begin by stating that there should not be any hazard out of which the ball cannot be extricated at the loss of one stroke, and that all hazards should be visible to the golfer when he stands at his ball before playing his stroke. A bunker that is not visible to the player is always more or less of a 'trap.' Sand bunkers are undoubtedly the most legitimate hazards. When there are natural bunkers, it may be possible to place the holes so that these can be made use of, but otherwise they must be formed, and in all cases they ought to be big enough and deep enough and broad enough to prevent the possibility of a ball either rolling through or jumping over. It should not be possible for a ball to lie in such a position in a bunker that a stroke at it cannot be made so as to play the ball out in one direction or another, and the corners should not therefore be sharp and angular, but rather rounded off. The hazard should be sharply defined, so that there can be no doubt as to whether or not a ball lies in it. When bunkers are made, it is very usual to form the soil taken out into a cop in front, or behind, and sometimes in the middle. When such a thing is done, the cop should not be made high but rather broad, and it should not have steep sides. Among various kinds of hazards are to be found walls, trees, water, fences and hedges, whins, etc. Trees are never a fair hazard if at all near the line of play, as a well-hit shot may be completely spoiled by catching in the branches. An occasional wall or fence or stream of water or pond to be crossed cannot always be avoided, but I do not recommend the making of such hazards merely as hazards.

The placing of hazards is a matter of great difficulty, and their positions should be such that a golfer who is playing a good game should never visit them. The positions should be varied. There should, for example, be at certain holes hazards that must be carried, and should be carried, from the tee; these should be placed at such distances from the teeing-grounds that, while a well-hit shot will carry them, a topped or half-topped stroke will get in. At other holes the hazards should be placed so as to punish badly played second strokes; at others, again, the hazards should guard the putting-greens in front, and there may also be some hazards placed behind the greens. In neither of these cases should the hazards be too near the green; in the former it should be possible to loft well over the hazard, and yet lie near the hole, and in the latter it should only be a ball much too strongly played that is punished. There is a great cry nowadays that every hole should have a hazard in front requiring to be lofted over, but I think it is possible to carry a system of this kind too far. It ties players down to pitching all their approaches instead of making them exercise their judgment as to whether the ball should be lofted or run up. No golfer will deny that there should be hazards in front of some holes, but I think that at others there should be a clear road, with hazards judiciously placed on either side to punish wild shots. To loft a ball with an iron is comparatively easy to any player except an absolute novice, but it is not so easy to keep to the proper course. Erratic play should always meet with punishment, and I would counsel hazards being laid down on each side, not of the putting-greens alone, but also of the line to the hole, to catch pulled or sliced balls. I know that a bunker on the line of play, and into which a good stroke may get, is frequently considered a trap; but this is an opinion which I cannot altogether endorse. If the bunker is visible to the player, and there is sufficient room to avoid it, it cannot properly be called a trap. Golf as a game of skill requires that a player should be able to place his ball; and if he sees the hazard, and knows there is the danger of getting in, the proper thing for him to do is to drive his ball to one side or other of the difficulty.

Although blind holes (*i.e.* holes at which the player does not see the flag) are objectionable, they cannot always be dispensed with; but an endeavour should be made to place the hole in such a position that it can be seen in playing the approach. Having to play a blind stroke through the green or from the tee is less objectionable than having to play a blind approach. In all cases, a guide-post should be placed to show the direction in which the ball is intended to be played, not necessarily in the direct line to the hole. The guide-post should indicate safety to the average player.

When the ground has to be cleared of whins, etc., they should be rooted up and not merely cut over. Whins are, I may mention, delicate of growth, and walking over soon kills them out.

When a new green is being formed, it is a mistake to do anything precipitately. Experience of the course will best show its capabilities and the proper position for holes, tees, and hazards.

After the links has been laid out it will be found that the upkeep of it requires much attention and care. The parts which suffer most from continuous play are the teeing-grounds, the places from whence approaches are played with iron clubs, and the putting-greens. Arrangements should be made for changing the places for teeing by shifting the tees back or forward, or by removing them to different sites. The only ways by which provision can be made for repairing the ground cut up by approaches are, either by moving the holes to different putting-greens, or by altering the course of the round. Moving the holes to other greens means keeping up a greater number of putting-greens, and it is not so effectual as 'changing the round.' I do not approve greatly of the plan of having relief greens, and would rather advocate the making of large greens, to enable the hole to be moved about from time to time as occasion requires; and I would also advocate the reversing of the round, to permit of the damage done by iron play being made good. A continual watch should always be kept on the links, and whenever divots are cut out by play, the hole should be at once repaired; but, in addition to this, the whole links should receive a thorough overhaul yearly at the end of each season.

Now, the best means of repairing links varies according to the nature of the turf and the subsoil. On heavy links the best material for filling up holes is sand – a handful placed in the hole, pressed down with the foot, and the repair is executed; the sand soon goes down and gets intermingled with the soil. On some greens, where the subsoil is fine sand which will walk solid, the same material may be used; while on others, where the sand is sharp, and of a loose, open nature, a hack is apt to spread, and soil is required to help to bind the sand together. It may be taken as a rule that, where binding together is required, soil cannot be dispensed with, and that where this is not necessary sand alone may be used. In illustration of this I may quote the case of two of the best known links, St Andrews and Musselburgh. On the former nothing but sand is used, with the best possible results; but the sand there is of such a nature that walking over it makes it firm and hard. On the other hand, at Musselburgh a small hack soon becomes, by repeated walking over, a small bunker; and the more sand is put on it, the bigger does the evil become, the sand on this green being much sharper and more of a gravelly nature; and when a hole has to be mended, it is necessary to use earth to help to bind the sand together. If the damage to any part of a golf-green is at all extensive, the only satisfactory remedy – and this is generally applicable – is turfing over the injured part.

With regard to putting-greens, sand may generally be freely used. There is no feeding in sand, and it helps to open up the ground and to make the grass less coarse and rough. A good coating of sand may, as a rule, be applied to almost any putting-green with excellent results, especially if the grass is too strong and luxuriant. If, however, the subsoil is sandy and poor, the green may require nourishment, and a dressing of sand and soil, or, in some cases, of the latter alone, will be beneficial. It is a help to a poor green on which the grass is thin to add fine lawn seeds to the top dressing; but it is useless to sow grass seeds on the top of sand, as the heat of the sand seems to burn the seeds up. The proper course is to top-dress, then to sow, and thereafter to sprinkle again, taking care that in no case is the top-dressing too heavily applied. I have seen bone dust and bone meal and also artificial manures, and even stable manure, put through a riddle, applied to poor greens with good results. Nitre ammonia and such forcing substances should never be used, because they have the effect of forcing a growth of grass at the expense of the roots; and what is required on a putting-green is a thick sole, not a crop of grass.

Judicious rolling and cutting are of the utmost advantage. Rolling, however, requires to be carefully done and its results studied; the roller should not be too heavy, and rolling should never be allowed to have the effect of caking the green and rendering the grass root-bound. A light roller should be used as frequently as may be required. I have known excellent putting-greens completely spoiled by the use of a heavy horse-roller applied to save the expense of employing men to draw a light one. Some greens – new greens of a loose, spongy nature – require a heavy roller to bring them into subjection; but I am speaking of greens that have been brought into condition. When a horse-roller is used, the feet of the horse should be encased in 'boots,' to prevent the iron shoes injuring the green.

A very important matter frequently neglected is the position and cutting of the hole. The hole should always be placed on a fairly level piece of ground on the putting-green – never on a steep slope; and care should be taken to see that the hole is cut the exact size, 4¼ ins. in diameter and 4 ins. deep at least. It is usual to place a lining in the hole to prevent the edges being worn away, and the 4¼ ins. must of course be measured inside the lining. The lining should not be sunk too far beneath the surface of the ground, because if this is done the top edge becomes worn away by the rubbing of the flag-stick against it, thus allowing a ball which would otherwise have rolled past to fall in. The hole cutter and the tins should fit one another. I have seen holes cut with too small a cutter and the tin thereafter hammered in, the result being that the surrounding green buckled up slightly, forming a ridge round the hole. This frequently accounts for balls just sticking on the lip of the hole when they ought to have gone down. I have seen greens, too, where the lining of the holes, instead of being thin, was quite thick – about the sixteenth part of an inch, perhaps – with the top bevelled off; this is most objectionable, because if this kind of' 'tin' is at all near the surface, a ball played on the back of the hole will not go down, but will strike the bevel edge and jump out. It is the duty of those in charge of the green to see that such evils are avoided. The lining should be thin galvanised iron, made perfectly round, and measuring 4¼ inches inside diameter. The usual 'tin' is a side lining only, with no bottom; but there has recently been introduced a tin with a bottom, a small hole being left for the flag-stick to go through. The advantage of such a tin is that the ball is kept clean, and that the flag-stick stands – when properly put in – upright in the hole, thus saving the edges of the turf. Its disadvantage, however, lies in the fact that unless the hole is cut the exact depth of the tin – which is by no means an easy thing to do – either it has to be deepened to sink the tin sufficiently, or, if it is cut too deep, the tin, by the pin being carelessly put in, and striking the bottom, is knocked down too far to be a protection to the edges of the turf. The hole should be cut straight down and the tin inserted and pushed into position, so that the upper edge is from half an inch to a quarter of an inch below the surface of the ground, depending upon the firmness or looseness of the soil. After the tin is placed in position, the ground should be firmly batted down with the back of a spade, and the top edge of the hole trimmed up. When finished, the depth should be at least 4 inches. This matter of depth is a point not always attended to. In selecting a spot for the hole, care should be taken to see that the grass is properly trimmed round about, so that no strong blade is left which might turn a ball coming into contact with it. Heavy flagsticks are a frequent source of injury to holes. Players are apt to put them carelessly into the hole, and the pressure against the sides breaks the green and enlarges the hole. The deeper the hole is, the less danger there is of this happening, and hence the hole should always be of a good depth.

On eighteen-hole courses it is usual to have the flags of different colours for the outgoing and the incoming nine holes. Red going out and white coming in, or vice versa, these colours showing up best against the green. The original idea was to prevent confusion to players, when the outgoing and incoming putting-greens lay near each other; but nowadays, even in cases where there is no risk of confusion, the custom is observed. The best mode of marking the teeing-grounds is by white discs, fastened into the ground with long pins through the centre, one at each end of the teeing-ground, in a line at right angles to the direction of play.

The edges of bunkers get broken down by players walking over them, and the proper cure is to repair them by putting in turfs, laid one on the top of the other. Wood is sometimes used, but it is objectionable in this, that a ball may hit the wood and jump out of the hazard. All large stones, etc., should be taken out of bunkers, as they are not only unfair, but apt to cause injury to clubs. The raking of bunkers is sometimes practised, but it is not a thing I am in favour of. A ball lying on the raked surface will be teed, and may possibly be driven as far as if lying on grass, thus frustrating the very purpose the hazard was intended to accomplish. Moreover, in competitions for example, the first couples get the best of the bunkers, as each succeeding couple, if they get in, walk the sand into holes. On greens where the sand walks solid, the bunkers should be dug up. If the sides are steep, it is a good plan to put in a short ladder, or a few steps, to save the edges from being broken down by players clambering up.

For keeping down the grass through the course, nothing can be better than grazing with sheep. Some clubs look for a good revenue from this, but golf and grazing are not compatible. If the ground be kept in trim for golf, there is little grazing to be got, and if the grazing is good, it means that the grass is too long for golf. Grazing by sheep is – irrespective of the rent it produces – the best mode of keeping down superfluous grass, and it has the effect of enriching the ground when poor. Cattle should not be permitted to graze for obvious reasons, and horses cut up the ground. But if the growth of grass is very luxuriant, grazing may not be sufficient, and it may be necessary to resort to cutting the whole green – an expensive proceeding. The golfers should always endeavour to get the grazing into their own hands, so as to be able to regulate the putting on or the taking off of sheep, and the number to be grazed. If there is a separate grazing tenant who is not under the control of the golfers, he may give a good deal of trouble, and cause much annoyance.

Walking over a green improves it very much, and consolidates it. It wears away the rough grass, which is replaced by an after-growth of short turf, and it is much more efficacious than cutting. When a new green is opened, give it plenty of walking over and play to tramp it down, before proceeding to incur expense in the way of cutting.

CHAPTER ELEVEN

The Laws of Golf

THE ROYAL AND ANCIENT Golf Club of St Andrews are generally recognised to be the lawgivers of the game, and the St
Andrews Rules are invariably adopted by other clubs. It is
somewhat unfortunate, however, that the rules which they
have framed are not sufficiently comprehensive, nor are they
apparently intended to be applicable to all links on which golf
is played; and it would almost seem as if they were drawn up
with reference to St Andrews Links alone. The result of this is,
that while these rules are adopted by other clubs, they frequently require modification to suit local requirements, and it
cannot therefore be said that the code of laws as it stands is
always of general application. The only other club which has
framed a set of rules for itself is the Royal Wimbledon Golf
Club; but I am not aware that their rules are adopted by
another club in preference to the St Andrews code, and such a
proceeding would in Scotland be deemed little short of sacri-
lege. As a matter of fact, while both codes have their good and
bad points, I recommend the adoption of the St Andrews
Rules, subject to such additional local rules as may be necessary. This on the ground that they are invariably accepted, and
it is desirable that till clubs should, as far as practicable, play
under the same Rules. The Wimbledon Rules, however, will be
found printed after the St Andrews Rules, so that the two
codes can easily be compared. A table showing the points of
difference between them is also given.

One can hardly take up a sporting newspaper which
devotes a column to golf without being astonished by seeing
the number of inquiries on the subject of the rules; and with
the view of making them more easily understood by those who
have not had the advantage of previous acquaintance with for-

mer rules, and the customs of golf, I have appended to each rule such observations thereon as occur to me may be of service. These notes are printed in smaller type, to distinguish them from the actual rules.

I would repeat the remark already made, that a thorough knowledge of the laws of the game is essential for all who profess to be golfers.

RULES FOR THE GAME OF GOLF

Adopted by the Royal and Ancient Golf Club of St Andrews on 29 September 1891, as amended on 1 May 1895.

1. The game of golf is played by two or more sides, each playing its own ball. A side may consist of one or more persons.

2. The game consists in each side playing a ball from a tee into a hole by successive strokes, and the hole is won by the side holing its ball in the fewest strokes, except as otherwise provided for in the rules. If two sides hole out in the same number of strokes, the hole is halved.

These two rules are explanatory of the game.

3. The teeing-ground shall be indicated by two marks placed in a line at right angles to the course, and the player shall not tee in front of, nor on either side of, these marks, nor more than two club-lengths behind them. A ball played from outside the limits of the teeing-ground, as thus defined, may be recalled by the opposite side.

The hole shall be 4¼ inches in diameter, and at least 4 inches deep.

The proper method of indicating the teeing-ground is as above provided. On some courses, however, the teeing-grounds are indicated by four marks – two in front and two behind – in which case the ball must be teed within the space so marked off, as the two latter marks are intended to show the limit of two club-lengths, behind which the ball cannot be teed. If a ball is teed outside of the defined limits, the proper and sportsmanlike course for the opponent to adopt is to demand that the ball be brought within the limits before the stroke is played. At the same time the above is the rule (which I have frequently seen enforced), and the opponent is entitled, if he so choose, to recall a ball driven from outside the teeing-ground. This means that he may insist on another ball being played from within the proper place, but of course the playing of the first ball which is recalled does not count as a stroke. The size of the hole should be measured inside any lining which may be placed in it.

4. The ball must be fairly struck at, and not pushed, scraped, or spooned, under penalty of the loss of the hole. Any movement of the club which is intended to strike the ball is a stroke.

The ball must of course be struck at with a golf-club. It is not allowable to play a ball with the shaft of a club as with a billiard-cue, nor is it allowable to place the club-head close down beside the ball and lift it forward, as I have seen done when the ball lay in a bunker. The ball *must be struck*. It is counted a stroke if the ball be struck at, even if it be not actually touched or moved, either through the club hitting the ground behind the ball, or through swinging the club right over the top of it.

5. The game commences by each side playing a ball from the first teeing-ground. In a match with two or more on a side, the partners shall strike off alternately from the tees, and shall strike alternately during the play of the hole.

The players who are to strike against each other shall be named at starting, and shall continue in the same order during the match.

The player who shall play first on each side shall be named by his own side.

In case of failure to agree, it shall be settled by lot or toss which side shall have the option of leading.

The last sentence of the first paragraph and the second and third paragraphs refer to foursome play. The last paragraph applies to all matches. If the parties cannot agree which is to have the honour, it shall be settled by lot. The custom used to be to give the first honour to the captain of the club, or oldest member of the club playing in the match.

6. If a player shall play when his partner should have done so, his side shall lose the hole, except in the case of the tee-shot, when the stroke may be recalled at the option of the opponents.

As before pointed out, the recalled stroke is not counted.

7. The side winning a hole shall lead in starting for the next hole, and may recall the opponent's stroke should he play out of order. This privilege is called the 'honour.' On starting for a new match, the winner of the long match in the previous round is entitled to the 'honour.' Should the first match have been halved, the winner of the last hole gained is entitled to the 'honour.'

The 'long match' means the previous match, irrespective of the bye which may have remained to play after the match was decided. Thus a golfer wins his match by four up and three to play, but loses all the remaining three holes, which in all probability will be played as a bye. Notwithstanding his losing the bye, he – as the winner of the match (or the long match) – is entitled to the honour in starting for a new round.

8. One round of the links – generally eighteen holes – is a match, unless otherwise agreed upon. The match is won by the side which gets more holes ahead than there remain holes to be played, or by the side winning the last hole when the match was all even at the second last hole. If both sides have won the same number, it is a halved match.

9. After the balls are struck from the tee, the ball furthest from the hole to which the parties are playing shall be played first, except as otherwise provided for in the rules. Should the wrong side play first, the opponent may recall the stroke before his side has played.

Observe the wording of the first part of this rule. Suppose the player who has the honour (1) misses the globe altogether, or (2) that his ball after being driven hits a stone or a post, or some obstruction, and rebounds to a distance behind the teeing-ground, he does not immediately play a second stroke; he must allow his opponent to play his tee-shot, the like, and the first player then plays the odd. 'Except as otherwise provided for in the rules' – see Rule 32 and Special Rules for Medal Play, 9. As before explained, the recalled stroke is not counted.

10. Unless with the opponent's consent, a ball struck from the tee shall not be changed, touched, or moved before the hole is played out, under the penalty of one stroke, except as otherwise provided for in the rules.

See Rules 13, 17, 20, 21, 22, 32, 36, 38; Special Rules for Medal Play, 8 and 9.

11. In playing through the green, all *loose* impediments, within a club-length of a ball which is not lying in or touching a hazard, may be removed, but loose impediments which are more than a club-length from the ball shall not be removed under the penalty of one stroke.

Compare with Rules 30 and 31, also with Rule 15. This rule only applies to 'loose impediments.'

12. Before striking at the ball, the player shall not move, bend, or break anything fixed or growing near the ball, except in the act of placing his feet on the ground for the purpose of addressing the ball, and in soling his club to address the ball, under the penalty of the loss of the hole, except as provided for in Rule 18.

Through the green the natural lie of the ball must not be improved in any way. The club may be soled, but this must not be done in such a way as to contravene the first part of the rule.

13. A ball stuck fast in wet ground or sand may be taken out and replaced loosely in the hole which it has made.

This only applies to *wet* ground or sand, and the ball must be replaced in the hole; the hole cannot be closed and the ball placed on the top.

14. When a ball lies in or touches a hazard, the club shall not touch the ground, nor shall anything be touched or moved before the player strikes at the ball except that the player may place his feet firmly on the ground for the purpose of address-ing the ball, under the penalty of the loss of the hole. *But if in the backward or in the downward swing any grass, bent, whin, or other growing substance, or the side of a bunker, a wall, a paling, or other immovable obstacle be touched, no penalty shall be incurred.*

The italics are mine. This latter part of the rule was added at a meet-ing of the Royal and Ancient Golf Club held on 1 May 1895. The whole rule is one of the most important in the code. It expressly prohibits any-thing that would in the slightest degree improve the position of a ball in a hazard. When the ball gets into 'fog, bent, whins, etc.,' Rule 18 must be read in conjunction with the above, but the player is not thereby entitled to put aside the whins, etc., to enable a better stroke to be made. The whins, etc., must not be touched (save with the object of allowing the ball to be seen) until in the act of striking.

15. A 'hazard' shall be any bunker of whatever nature: water, sand, loose earth, mole-hills, paths, roads or railways, whins, bushes, rushes, rabbit-scrapes, fences, ditches, or any-thing which is not the ordinary green of the course, except sand blown on to the grass by wind, or sprinkled on grass for the preservation of the links, or snow or ice, or bare patches on the course.

This rule consists of two parts, the first specific and the second gen-eral; but the specific hazards mentioned do not limit the definition of hazards to those specifically enumerated. It would seem that blown sand, snow, or ice can be regarded as loose impediments within the meaning of Rule 11, and in this case the sand, etc., within a club-length of the ball can be brushed away, which practically results in leaving the ball teed. I hardly think, however, that this can have been intended to be the mean-ing of the rule, but rather that it was merely meant to permit of the club being soled when the ball lies on such sand, etc. With reference to this, see Rule 34, which permits sand, etc., to be removed on the putting-green.

Here is an interesting question upon which the rule gives no direct information. Suppose a large bunker with a fair-sized patch of grass in the centre of it. Is a ball lying on this patch of grass in a hazard or not? My own view is that it is not. The ball is either in the bunker or it is not, and grass is not a bunker; therefore the ball is not in the hazard. I am aware, however, that the point is considered debatable.

16. A player or a player's caddie shall not press down or remove any irregularities of surface near the ball, except at the teeing-ground, under the penalty of the loss of the hole.

At the teeing-ground anything can be done to improve the tee, and it is quite usual to press down with the foot the grass behind the ball; but this cannot be done at any other place, nor can the lie of the ball through the green be improved by pressing the club down behind the ball or otherwise.

17. If any vessel, wheel-barrow, tool, roller, grass-cutter, box, or other similar obstruction has been placed upon the course, such obstruction may be removed. A ball lying on or touching such obstruction, or on clothes, or nets, or on ground under repair or temporarily covered up or opened, may be lifted and dropped at the nearest point of the course, but a ball lifted in a hazard shall be dropped in the hazard. A ball lying in a golf-hole or flag-hole may be lifted and dropped not more than a club-length behind such hole.

The theory of the rule is that there should not be any 'vessels, etc.' on the links in the player's way. Ground under repair should be marked off and indicated; it frequently happens that turf has been lifted from ground off the line of play, but on to which erratic players manage to drive, and the rule cannot be said to be intended to cover this contingency, because, if the ground is off the line, the player has no business to be there, and he is only receiving his deserts by finding himself in difficulties.

It is part of the unwritten laws of golf that balls shall not be played off a putting-green, and where a ball does happen to get on to the wrong putting-green, requiring to be played off, it is invariably lifted and dropped on the nearest part of the course. A rule for this, adopted by many clubs, is given at the end of this code.

18. When a ball is completely covered with fog, bent,

whins, etc., only so much thereof shall be set aside as that the player shall have a view of his ball before he plays, whether in a line with the hole or otherwise.

Observe the latter part of the rule. The player is not entitled to improve his position. He is only entitled to see where his ball lies before striking at it.

19. When a ball is to be dropped, the player shall drop it. He shall front the hole, stand erect behind the hazard, keep the spot from which the ball was lifted (or in the case of running water, the spot at which it entered) in a line between him and the hole, and drop the ball behind him from his head, standing as far behind the hazard as he may please.

The player must himself drop it, not his caddie nor his partner. Care should be taken that the ball drops clear of a hazard, because when the ball has been dropped it is in play and cannot be again touched except under the Rules, and, if again liftable, subject to any fresh penalty that may be exigible.

20. When the balls in play lie within six inches of each other – measured from their nearest points – the ball nearer the hole shall be lifted until the other is played, and shall then be replaced as nearly as possible in its original position. Should the ball further from the hole be accidentally moved in so doing, it shall be replaced. Should the lie of the lifted ball be altered by the opponent in playing, it may be placed in a lie near to, and as nearly as possible similar to, that from which it was lifted.

Suppose that, after the players have driven off, both balls lie together, almost touching each other; if the ball nearer the hole were lifted, and the opponent in playing the other ball took it heavy and cut out a divot of turf, to replace the lifted ball on the exact spot where it originally lay would possibly mean placing it in a hole. I have actually seen such a case happen, and it is to meet such a contingency that this rule is enacted. Under it the lifted ball would not be replaced in the hole, but 'in a lie near to, and as nearly as possible similar to, that from which it was lifted.'

21. If the ball lie or be lost in water, the player may drop a ball, under the penalty of one stroke.

Water means any water on the course, either streams or ponds or pools formed by rain. It is optional to the player either to lift or to play, and he may sometimes prefer to do the latter when the ball lies in a small shallow rain-formed pool. The actual working out of this rule may, and sometimes does, lead to anomalies, as, for instance, when the water is in a hazard. Two balls may be lying in the same hazard within a couple of yards of one another, the one in water and the other not, the first can be lifted, and taken out of the hazard under the above rule, subject to the penalty of a stroke, while the other would require to be played as it lay or the hole given up, or, in a stroke competition, dealt with under Special Rules for Medal Play, 8.

22. Whatever happens by accident to a ball *in motion*, such as its being deflected or stopped by any agency outside the match, or by the fore-caddie, is a 'rub of the green,' and the ball shall be played from where it lies. Should a ball lodge in anything moving, such ball, or if it cannot be recovered, another ball, shall be dropped as nearly as possible at the spot where the object was when the ball lodged in it. But if a ball at rest be displaced by any agency outside the match, the player shall drop it or another ball as nearly as possible at the spot where it lay. On the putting-green the ball may be replaced by hand.

23. If the player's ball strike, or be accidentally moved by an opponent or an opponent's caddie or clubs, the opponent loses the hole.

24. If the player's ball strike, or be stopped by himself or his partner, or either of their caddies or clubs, or if, while in the act of playing, the player strike the ball twice, his side loses the hole.

It is difficult for any one but the player to say if a ball is struck twice in the act of making a stroke. Striking twice occurs sometimes in putting when the ball lies in a 'nick' on the green – the putter hits the ball, which thereupon jumps up off the face of the nick and the putter again hits it in the follow-through. It may also happen in playing a full stroke with an iron club through the ball being hit first with the hose and afterwards with the blade of the club, but the movements are so quick as to defy detection except by the sound, and can only be proved by examining the club used and seeing if there are two distinct marks of impact of the ball on it.

25. If the player when not making a stroke, or his partner or either of their caddies touch their side's ball, except at the tee, so as to move it, or by touching anything cause it to move, the penalty is one stroke.

26. A ball is considered to have been moved if it leave its original position in the least degree and stop in another; but if a player touch his ball and thereby cause it to oscillate, without causing it to leave its original position, it is not moved in the sense of Rule 25.

The most fruitful source of moving balls is carelessness in addressing them, especially when the ball lies either on very keen ground or in long grass.

27. A player's side loses a stroke if he play the opponent's ball, unless (1) the opponent then play the player's ball, whereby the penalty is cancelled and the hole must be played out with the balls thus exchanged, or (2) the mistake occur through wrong information given by the opponent, in which case the mistake, if discovered before the opponent has played, must be rectified by placing a ball as nearly as possible where the opponent's ball lay.

If it be discovered before either side has struck off at the tee that one side has played out the previous hole with the ball of a party not engaged in the match, that side loses that hole.

There is no excuse for a player not knowing his own ball. If he finds any difficulty about it, he should mark his ball to prevent all question. It must be remembered that he is not entitled to lift a ball to examine it unless with his opponent's consent. See Rule 10.

28. If a ball be lost, the player's side loses the hole. A ball shall be held as lost if it be not found within five minutes after the search is begun.

I apprehend that for the purposes of this rule a ball is lost if it cannot be gathered, even though it can be seen, as, for instance, in the case of a ball down a rabbit-hole, visible, yet out of reach.

29. A ball must be played wherever it lies, or the hole given up, except as otherwise provided for in the Rules.

Although the St Andrews Rules say nothing about this, it is usual for clubs to make a local rule about rabbit holes and scrapes where it is necessary. Such a rule is given at the end of this code.

30. The term 'putting-green' shall mean the ground within twenty yards of the hole, excepting hazards.

31. All loose impediments may be removed from the putting-green, except the opponent's ball when at a greater distance from the player's than six inches.

Loose impediments. Nothing fixed or growing can be removed.

32. In a match of three or more sides, a ball in any degree lying between the player and the hole must be lifted, or, if on the putting-green, holed out.

Stymies are not played in three-ball matches.

33. When a ball is on the putting-green, no mark shall be placed, nor line drawn as a guide. The line to the hole may be pointed out, but the person doing so may not touch the ground with the hand or club.

The player may have his own or his partner's caddie to stand at the hole, but none of the players or their caddies may move so as to shield the ball from, or expose it to, the wind.

The penalty for any breach of this rule is the loss of the

THE GAME OF GOLF

hole.

The line to the hole must not be touched. The second paragraph of the rule makes it advisable that the players and their caddies shall not move when a putt is being played, or until the ball has ceased to roll.

34. The player or his caddie may remove (but not press down) sand, earth, worm-casts, or snow lying around the hole or on the line of his putt. This shall be done by brushing lightly with the hand only across the putt and not along it. Dung may be removed to a side by an iron club, but the club must not be laid with more than its own weight upon the ground. The putting-line must not be touched by club, hand, or foot, except as above authorised, or immediately in front of the ball in the act of addressing it, under the penalty of the loss of the hole.

Although a matter of doubt at one time, it is now settled that the last sentence of this rule does not prevent the player from placing his putter in front of his ball with the view of adjusting the face of the club before playing.

35. Either side is entitled to have the flag-stick removed when approaching the hole. If the ball rest against the flag-stick when in the hole, the player shall be entitled to remove the stick, and if the ball fall in, it shall be considered as holed out in the previous stroke.

See Etiquette of Golf, Rule 8.

36. A player shall not play until the opponent's ball shall have ceased to roll, under the penalty of one stroke. Should the player's ball knock in the opponent's ball, the latter shall be counted as holed out in the previous stroke. If in playing the player's ball displace the opponent's ball, the opponent shall have the option of replacing it.

37. A player shall not ask for advice, nor be knowingly

advised about the game by word, look, or gesture from any one except his own caddie, or his partner or partner's caddie, under the penalty of the loss of the hole.

I am afraid that this rule is not so strictly observed as it should be. A friend walking round with a match too often is asked for and gives advice in defiance of the strict law.

38. If a ball split into separate pieces, another ball may be put down where the largest portion lies, or if two pieces are apparently of equal size, it may be put where either piece lies, at the option of the player. If a ball crack or become unplayable, the player may change it, on intimating to his opponent his intention to do so.

39. A penalty stroke shall not be counted the stroke of a player, and shall not affect the rotation of play.

40. Should any dispute arise on any point, the players have the right of determining the party or parties to whom the dispute shall be referred; but should they not agree, either party may refer it to the Green Committee of the green where the dispute occurs, and their decision shall be final. Should the dispute not be covered by the Rules of Golf the arbiters must decide it by equity.

The Rules do not provide for any mode of protest in the event of dispute between players. Suppose, for example, a ball lies on a place which the player of the ball maintains is not a hazard, while his opponent as stoutly maintains it is. What is to be done? The question is one which obviously cannot wait the decision of a non-present referee or of a Green Committee. There are two courses open to the aggrieved party; one is to lift his ball and claim the hole if the player breaks the Rules by grounding his club in the disputed ground or otherwise, and the other is to play out the hole. If he does the first he runs the risk of its being held that the ground is not a hazard, and he thereby loses a hole he might otherwise have won or halved; and if he adopts the alternative course he may be met with the argument that he had played out the hole and debarred himself from referring the matter in dispute. I think it is unfortunate that the Rules are silent on this subject, and in the event of dispute arising I would recommend the player who thinks the Rules have been broken to play out the hole under protest, intimated to his opponent. In competitions each player is supposed to know the Rules, and to play accordingly; it is not for his partner, who plays with him – and whose duty it is to see that the Rules are observed – to insist on the latter's interpretation being acted on. If such partner notices what he considers a contravention of the Rules, his proper course is to report accordingly when the cards are returned, and let the Committee decide.

SPECIAL RULES OF MEDAL PLAY

(1.) In club competitions, the competitor doing the stipulated course in fewest strokes shall be the winner.

(2.) If the lowest score be made by two or more competitors, the ties shall be decided by another round to be played either on the same or on any other day as the Captain, or, in his absence, the Secretary shall direct.

(3.) New holes shall be made for the Medal Round, and thereafter no member shall play any stroke on a putting-green before competing.

The application of this rule is much more sweeping than most players imagine. No stroke on any putting-green can be played before the competition without rendering the player liable to disqualification.

(4.) The scores shall be kept by a special marker, or by the competitors noting each other's scores. The scores marked shall be checked at the finish of each hole. On completion of the course, the score of the player shall be signed by the person keeping the score and handed to the Secretary.

In amateur competitions it is usual for the competitors playing together to mark each other's score. In open competitions markers usually accompany the couples.

(5.) If a ball be lost, the player shall return as nearly as possible to the spot where the ball was struck, tee another ball, and lose a stroke. If the lost ball be found before he has struck the other ball, the first shall continue in play.

This rule about a lost ball puzzles a number of players. The penalty of a stroke and distance is equivalent to a penalty of two strokes, and it works out thus: the stroke played from which the ball is lost is the first, the penalty stroke counts as the second, and the stroke which the player makes in playing the fresh ball counts as the third. The player is therefore in much the same position with his third stroke as he would have been with his first had he played it properly.

(6.) If the player's ball strike himself, or his clubs, or caddie, or if, in the act of playing, the player strike the ball twice, the penalty shall be one stroke.

(7.) If a competitor's ball strike the other player, or his clubs or caddie, it is a 'rub of the green' and the ball shall be played from where it lies.

(8.) A ball may, under a penalty of two strokes, be lifted out of a difficulty of any description, and be teed behind same.

This is a most important rule in medal competitions, and has no parallel in match play. It is better to lift a ball out of a hazard, and count two strokes for so doing, than to hammer away fruitlessly at the ball. But it is optional to the player either to lift or to play the ball.

(9.) All balls shall be holed out, and when play is on the putting-green, the flag shall be removed, and the competitor whose ball is nearest the hole shall have the option of holing out first, or of lifting his ball, if it be in such a position that it might, if left, give an advantage to the other competitor. Throughout the green a competitor can have the other competitor's ball lifted, if he find that it interferes with his stroke.

All balls must be holed out, even a ball lying within an inch of the hole. This rule prevents the application to medal competitions of Rule 36, as to a ball being knocked into the hole; if this happens the ball must be replaced and holed out. One competitor is not entitled to give another the advantage of leaving his ball lying near the hole to make it bigger. If his ball be in such a position that it might give an advantage to the other competitor, it must be holed out first or lifted.

(10.) A competitor may not play with a professional, and he may not receive advice from any one but his caddie.

A fore-caddie may be employed.

(11.) Competitors may not discontinue play because of bad weather.

(12.) The penalty for a breach of any rule shall be disqualification.

(13.) Any dispute regarding the play shall be determined by the Green Committee.

(14.) The ordinary Rules of Golf, so far as they are not at variance with these special rules, shall apply to medal play.

ETIQUETTE OF GOLF

It is doubtful how far the following injunctions are obligatory as laws of the game, except by courtesy, but there is no doubt that they ought to be observed, and there is also no doubt that custom authorises the enforcing of the most of them, and that in one instance, at least, by very drastic measures.

The following customs belong to the established Etiquette of Golf and should be observed by all golfers.

1. No player, caddie, or onlooker should move or talk during a stroke.

2. No player should play from the tee until the party in front have played their second strokes and are out of range, nor play to the putting-green till the party in front have holed out and moved away.

There is no rule more religiously and jealously enforced than this one, and disregard of it is held as entitling the party played into to drive back the offender's ball. Of course no one would resort to this extreme measure unless the provocation were great and the breach of etiquette repeated more than once after due remonstrance.

3. The player who leads from the tee should be allowed to play before his opponent tees his ball.

The reason for this is that the second ball may catch the eye of the player who is about to drive, and so interfere with his stroke.

4. Players who have holed out should not try their putts over again when other players are following them.

5. Players looking for a lost ball must allow any other match coming up to pass them.

The match behind cannot be asked to wait until the players looking for the lost ball have exhausted the statutory limit of time under Rule 28. The following couples are entitled to go on without pause, and it is only courteous for the couple causing the delay to permit of this without cavil.

6. A party playing three or more balls must allow a two-ball match to pass them.

The two-ball match must have started and played in regular course to entitle them to pass the three ball-match. A three-ball match should not be played on a busy green except by first-class golfers, and then only with consent of the following couples. Good golfers playing a three-ball match do not, as a rule, block or keep back the succeeding couples.

7. A party playing a shorter round must allow a two-ball match playing the whole round to pass them.

8. A player should not putt at the hole when the flag is in it.

9. The reckoning of the strokes is kept by the terms 'the odd,' 'two more,' 'three more,' etc., and 'one off three,' 'one off two,' 'the like.' The reckoning of the holes is kept by the terms so many 'holes up,' or 'all even,' and so many 'to play.'

10. Turf cut or displaced by a stroke in playing should be at once replaced.

LOCAL RULES FOR ST ANDREWS LINKS

1. When the Green Committee consider it necessary, a telegraph board shall be used to give the numbers for starting.

2. If the ball lie in any position in the Swilcan Burn, whether in water or not, the player may drop it, or if it cannot

THE GAME OF GOLF

be recovered, another ball may be dropped on the line where it entered the burn, on the opposite side to the hole to that to which he is playing, under the penalty of one stroke.

3. Should a ball be driven into the water of the Eden at the high hole, or into the sea at the first hole, the ball, or, if it cannot be recovered, another ball, shall be teed a club-length in front of either river or sea near the spot where it entered, under the penalty of one stroke.

4. A ball in the enclosure (between the road and dyke holes) called the station-master's garden shall be a lost ball.

5. If a ball lie within two yards of a fixed seat, it may be lifted and dropped two yards to the side of the seat farthest from the hole.

6. Any dispute respecting the play shall be determined by the Green Committee.

7. Competitions for the Spring and Autumn Medals of the club (with the exception of the George Glennie Medal) shall be decided by playing one round of the links, and the competitor doing it in fewest strokes shall be the winner.

8. The order of starting for the Spring and Autumn Medals will be balloted for on the previous evening, and intending competitors must give in their names to the Secretary not later than five o'clock on the previous evening. Any competitor not at the teeing-ground when his number is called shall be disqualified, unless it be proved to the satisfaction of the Green Committee or Secretary that he has a valid excuse, such as serious temporary illness, a train late, or such like, in which case he may be allowed to compete, and, if allowed, shall be placed at the bottom of the list. The absent competitor's partner may start in his proper turn, provided he get another player to play with him.

9. Competitors for medals or prizes are not allowed to delay starting on account of bad weather, but must strike off immediately after the preceding party has crossed the burn, and, after they have started, are not allowed to take shelter, but must complete their round in the order of their start. In cases of stoppage by accident, or severe temporary illness, the

Green Committee may allow a competitor to resume play.

10. All private matches must be delayed till the last medal competitors have holed out at the first hole.

LENGTH OF HOLES ON ST ANDREWS LINKS

Out		In	
1st Hole	352 yards	1st Hole	290 yards
2nd "	417 "	2nd "	150 "
3rd "	335 "	3rd "	333 "
4th "	367 "	4th "	385 "
5th "	516 "	5th "	475 "
6th "	359 "	6th "	375 "
7th "	340 "	7th "	334 "
8th "	170 "	8th "	461 "
9th "	277 "	9th "	387 "
	3,133 "		3,190 "

TABLE SHOWING AT WHAT HOLES STROKES ARE TO BE TAKEN IN THE QUEEN VICTORIA JUBILEE VASE (HANDICAP) TOURNAMENT OF THE ROYAL AND ANCIENT GOLF CLUB OF ST ANDREWS

1	8																
2	5	11															
3	2	8	14														
4	3	7	11	15													
5	2	5	8	12	16												
6	2	5	8	11	14	17											
7	2	5	8	11	13	16	18										
8	2	4	6	8	11	13	15	17									
9	2	4	6	8	10	12	14	16	18								
10	1	3	5	7	9	10	11	13	15	17							
11	1	3	4	6	7	9	10	12	14	15	17						
12	1	3	4	6	7	9	10	12	13	15	16	18					
13	1	2	4	6	8	9	11	12	14	15	16	17	18				
14	1	2	3	5	6	8	9	10	11	13	14	16	17	18			
15	1	2	3	5	6	7	8	9	10	11	13	14	16	17	18		
16	1	2	3	5	6	7	8	9	10	11	12	13	14	16	17	18	
17	1	2	3	4	5	6	7	8	9	10	11	13	14	15	16	17	18

INDEX TO RULES

NOTE – *This Index does not embrace the Etiquette of Golf nor the Local Rules for St Andrews Links*

(THE ITALICS REFER TO RULES FOR MEDAL PLAY)

The following rules, which are not in the St Andrews code, may be found useful:

If a ball lodge in a rabbit hole or scrape, the player may take it out and tee it a club-length behind the hazard, losing a stroke. If, however, the hole or scrape be in a hazard, the ball may be lifted and dropped behind, but not out of the hazard, under the same penalty. If a ball lodge in a rabbit-scrape on the putting-green, it may be taken out and placed behind, without any penalty.

In the event of any players causing undue delays, either in playing the game or otherwise, so that the hole in front of that to which they are playing is entirely unoccupied, the players immediately behind shall be entitled to pass such players, who shall be bound to permit this on being so required.

Balls shall not be driven or played from off any putting-green. When a ball lies on a putting-green on the way to another hole, it must be lifted and dropped beyond such putting-green, and not nearer the hole being played to, without a penalty.

RULES AND BYE-LAWS FOR THE GAME OF GOLF MADE BY THE ROYAL WIMBLEDON GOLF CLUB, 1883

RULES

MODE AND ORDER OF PLAYING THE GAME

1. The game of golf is played by two persons, or by four (two of a side playing alternately). It may also be played by three or more persons, each playing his own ball.

The game commences by each side playing off a ball from the starting-point called the 'teeing-ground.' In a match of four, those who are to play off and 'strike against' each other shall be named at starting.

The reckoning of the strokes is kept by the terms 'odds,' 'like,' 'two more,' 'one off two,' etc., and the hole is won by the player holing in the fewest strokes.

The party gaining the hole 'has the honour,' *i.e.* leads off for the next hole, and may recall his opponent's stroke should

he play out of order. On starting for a second match the winner of the previous match 'has the honour.' On starting for a
second round the winner of the 'long match' in the previous
round is entitled to the 'honour.' Should the first round have
been halved, the winner of the last hole 'has the honour.'

No player may play his tee ball until the party in front
have played their second strokes.

In match play, after the balls have been struck off, the ball
furthest from the hole to which the parties are playing must be
played first, or the opponent may recall the stroke.

In a three-ball match, should a ball in any degree interpose
on the putting-green between the player's ball and the hole, it
must be played first.

One round of the links is reckoned a match, unless otherwise stipulated.

If in a double match a player play out of his turn his side
loses the hole.

PLACE OF TEEING

2. The ball must be teed within the limits of the ground
marked out for the purpose, and not more than two club-
lengths behind the front line. In match play the penalty for the
infringement of this rule shall be the recall of the stroke at the
option of the opponent. In medal play the stroke must be
recalled, the penalty being the loss of the stroke.

A STROKE

3. The ball must be fairly struck, and not 'pushed,'
'scraped,' or 'spooned,' and any movement of the club, made
with the intention of striking at the ball, must be considered a
stroke.

CLUB BREAKING

4. If, in striking, the club break, it is a stroke, if the part of

the club remaining in the player's hand either strike the ground, touch the ball, or pass it. Should the club, in striking, catch in anything, such as a whin-branch or portion of paling, and break, it must be considered a stroke, even if the part remaining in the player's hand do not strike the ground, touch the ball, or pass it.

AGAINST CHANGING BALL

5. A ball struck off from the tee must not be changed, touched, or moved before the hole is played out, except in striking, and the cases specially provided for in the Rules. If the players are at a loss to know the one ball from the other, neither shall be lifted without the consent of both parties.

BALLS 'WITHIN SIX INCHES'

6. Whenever the balls lie within six inches of each other (the six inches to be measured from the inner surfaces), the ball nearest the hole must be lifted till the other has be to played, and then replaced as nearly as possible in its original position.

BALL IN WATER

7. If the ball lie in casual water on the course, the player may take it out, change the ball if he please, tee it, and play from behind the hazard, losing a stroke.

If the ball be in water in a hazard, or the water itself be a recognised hazard, it may be lifted and dropped behind the hazard, under the same penalty.

If the ball be seen to enter water from which it cannot be recovered, the penalty shall be the same as if recovered.

DROPPING BALL

8. In all cases where a ball is to be dropped, the player shall

front the hole to which he is playing, stand erect behind the hazard, and drop the ball behind him from his head, the spot at which the ball was found being kept between him and the hole.

BALL LOST

9. If the ball be lost, the player returns to the spot, as nearly as possible, from which the ball was struck, tees another ball, and loses a stroke.

If the ball be found before the party has struck the other ball, the first shall continue to be played.

Whenever the second ball is struck the first ball is out of play.

A player may not delay more than five minutes searching for a lost ball.

BALL SPLITTING

10. If a ball split into two or more pieces, a fresh ball may be put down where the largest portion of the ball was found; and if a ball be cracked the player may change it on intimating his intention of doing so to his opponent.

BAD-LYING BALL

11. No whins, bushes, ferns, rushes, grass, or moss shall be broken, bent, or trodden on, or adjusted in any way to enable the player to obtain a clearer view of his ball, or better swing, before playing; nor is it allowable to press down any irregularities of surface to improve the lie of the ball.

If the ball lie on sand, no impression may be made with the club, or otherwise, before striking.

LIFTABLE BALL

12. In match or medal play, a ball may, under a penalty of

two strokes, be lifted out of a difficulty of any description, and teed behind the hazard, the spot at which the ball was found being kept between the player and the hole. The hazard, in the case of whins or bushes, may be considered as the entire group.

When the ball lies on clothes, or in any of the holes made for golfing, flag-holes, rabbit-scrapes, or on ground under repair by the conservator of the course, it may be lifted, dropped behind the hazard, and played without a penalty. Should such a lie occur in a recognised hazard, the penalty for lifting shall be as in the previous paragraph.

LIFTABLE IMPEDIMENTS

13. All loose impediments, within a club-length of the ball when it lies on grass, either on or off the course, may be removed previous to playing, provided always that nothing be removed which would cause the ball to move out of its place.

IMPEDIMENTS NOT LIFTABLE

14. Nothing fixed or growing may be removed. A ball being in a hazard, nothing may be lifted.

'RUB OF THE GREEN', ETC.

15. Whatever happens by accident to a ball *in motion*, such as striking anything, must be reckoned 'a rub of the green,' and submitted to; but a ball *displaced* by any agency outside the match must be replaced, or another ball dropped, as near the spot as possible, without a penalty.

PLAYING WRONG BALL

16. If a player play his opponent's ball he loses the hole.

If this occur from wrong information given by the opponent, the penalty cannot be claimed; and should the mistake be discovered before the opponent has played the other ball, it must be rectified by the ball being replaced as nearly as possible where it lay.

If it be discovered, before either side has struck off for the next hole, that one of them has played out with a ball of a third party, he loses the hole.

BALLS EXCHANGED

17. If each side play the other's ball, the hole must be played out with the balls thus exchanged.

STRIKING OPPONENT'S BALL

18. If a player strike his opponent's ball with his foot, club, or otherwise, he loses the hole (except see Rules 16 and 17).

BALL STRIKING OPPONENT, ETC.

19. If the player's ball strike his opponent or his opponent's caddie or clubs, the opponent loses the hole.

BALL STRIKING PLAYER, ETC.

20. If, by accident, the player's ball strike himself or his caddie, or clubs, he loses a stroke.

STRIKING BALL TWICE

21. If, in the act of striking, the player strike the ball twice with his club, he loses a stroke.

TOUCHING OR DISPLACING BALL

22. If, after it has been played from the tee, the player, by accident, touch his ball with his foot, or any part of his body,

or displace it with his club, he loses a stroke.

APPROACHING THE PUTTING-GREEN

23. Players approaching a putting-green must wait until the party in front have holed out before playing on to the putting-green.

Either side is entitled to have the flag-stick removed.

CLEARING THE PUTTING-GREEN

24. All loose impediments, of whatever kind, may be removed from the putting-green if desired by the player, provided always that nothing be removed which would cause the ball to move out of its place. The putting-green includes all ground within twenty yards of the hole, with the exception of any portion which may be a hazard.

HOLING OUT THE BALL

25. No mark shall be placed or line drawn, either with the club or otherwise, to direct the ball to the hole.

A player or his caddie may remove sand, worm-earths, or such like, lying about the hole, but this must be done lightly with the hand. Except as above mentioned, or in the act of the player addressing himself to his ball, the putting-line must not be touched by the club, hand, or foot. If the player desire the line to the hole, it may be pointed out by a club shaft only.

If the ball rest against the flag-stick in the hole, the player shall be entitled to have the stick removed, and if the ball fall in, it shall be considered as holed out.

PARTIES PASSING EACH OTHER

26. A party, whether of two or four players, playing two balls, may pass parties playing three or more balls.

Players for medals and important prizes shall have precedence, both in starting and through the green, over parties playing ordinary matches.

CARE OF THE LINKS

27. The person appointed to take charge of the course shall make new holes when required, and in such places as to preserve the green in proper order. He shall mark out the tee-ing-grounds, carefully obliterating old marks, and shall carry out such instructions as he shall from time to time receive from the Green Committee.

Players having complaints to make regarding the state of the green, or suggestions thereon, should address them to the Committee, and not to the conservator of the links.

It is the duty of every player to replace, or see replaced, any portion of turf which may have been cut out in the act of play-ing; to have stones and other break-clubs cast off the course; and generally to conduce to the good preservation of the golf-ing-course and putting-green.

ASKING ADVICE

28. A player must not receive advice about the game, by word, look, or gesture, from any one except his own caddie, his partner's caddie, or his partner.

In medal play, a player may receive advice from his caddie alone.

DISPUTES

29. Any disputes respecting the play shall be referred to a party or parties mutually agreed upon, or to the Committee of the Club, either of whose decision shall be final.

BREACH OF RULES

30. In match play, where no special penalty for the

infringement of a rule is mentioned, the loss of the hole shall be the penalty.

In medal play the penalty shall be two strokes or disqualification, as determined by the Committee of the Club.

MEDAL PLAY – SPECIAL RULES

31. New holes shall always be made on the day the medal is played for, and no competitor may play at those holes before he starts for the prize, under the penalty of being disqualified for competing.

Before starting, each competitor must obtain from the Secretary a scoring-card; and, in the absence of a special marker, the players will note each other's score. They must satisfy themselves at the finish of each hole that their strokes have been accurately marked; and on completion of the round hand the card to the Secretary or his deputy.

All balls must be holed out.

No stymies are allowed.

The player nearest the hole must play first, or lift his ball, if it be in such a position that it might, if left, give an advantage to his partner.

If a player's ball be displaced by any agency except himself, or his caddie, it must be replaced as exactly as possible, without a penalty.

No competitor may play with a professional.

The ordinary rules of the game, so far as they are not at variance with these special rules, shall also be applicable on medal days.

BYE-LAWS

1. Balls lying on the tent rings or bare patches throughout the course, not being roads, paths, or recognised hazards, may be treated as balls lying on grass.

2. A ball may, under a penalty of a stroke, be lifted (*a*) from a whin, or grass among whins, and dropped; (*b*) from the gar-

THE GAME OF GOLF

dens, butts, enclosures, and new plantations, and dropped at a distance of two club-lengths from the enclosure, but so that it shall not settle nearer the hole than the spot from which it was lifted; should it do so it must be dropped again; (*c*) *in* the ravines, and dropped in the ravine behind the immediate hazard, or *from* ravines if played from tee and teed again on teeing-ground.

3. Any party having holed out at the green opposite either club-house, shall take precedence of any party waiting to strike off, such party waiting to follow next and so on alternately. No party having completed the round shall be entitled to benefit by this rule.

4. During the Autumn Competitions, between 1pm and 2.30pm, only those members playing for, or with a member playing for, the medals or other prizes shall be allowed to start, and the professional, or his deputy, shall be at the tee during this time to see that this bye-law is carried out.

5. On medal days no player shall start before the party in front have finished playing the first hole.

6. Players who have competed are bound, if necessary, to allow the use of their caddies to others who intend to compete.

ENCLOSURES

Ground enclosed by wire or other fencing at the third and fourteenth holes is out of play, and the ball must be lifted therefrom under penalty of one stroke, and dropped at a distance of two club-lengths from the side nearest the course, but not nearer the hole than the spot from which it is lifted. From all other enclosures for the preservation of the whins the ball must be lifted and dropped behind the hazard under penalty of one stroke (see Rule 8). If played from the tee into the old curling-pond, the ball may be teed again on teeing-ground under same penalty.

BALL ON PUTTING-GREENS

Except on medal days, a ball driven on to a putting-green (other than the one being played to) must be lifted and dropped off the green, but not nearer the hole, without penalty.

Note – Members are urgently requested to refrain from driving a ball when passers-by are within range, and to recollect that the ordinary custom of calling 'Fore!' adopted on most greens is not deemed sufficient at Wimbledon. The player must wait until passers-by have moved out of danger.

By Order

(signed) N R FOSTER
Hon. Sec.
THE CLUB HOUSE,
WIMBLEDON.

Recognised hazards where the ball may be lifted and teed behind under penalty of two strokes, and where the club may not be grounded, nor impediments lifted:

2nd	Hole.	Main road and roads to cottages.
3rd	”	Cart track from large butt.
6th	”	Carriage road, and ditch on other side of road.
7th & 9th	”	Paths in ravine, and on north and south sides of pond.
10th	”	Grassy road close to putting-green and trees.
15th	”	Sandy pot bunker.
16th	”	Carriage road.
17th	”	Sandy gravel before whins, and cart road.
18th	”	Main road to left, and cart road.

N.B. – Fifteenth hole: the water across main road is a hazard from which the ball may be lifted and dropped under penalty of one stroke.
Rushes all over course to be treated as whins (ball may be lifted and

dropped behind under penalty of one stroke).

From iron drain gratings (except on putting-green of sixth hole) the ball may be lifted and dropped behind without penalty.

MATCH PLAY ODDS

In singles, three-fourths of difference between handicap allowances.

In foursomes, three-eighths of difference between the aggregate handicap allowances on either side.

A half stroke, or over, shall count as one. Smaller fractions count as nothing.

Diffe-rence	Strokes in		Diffe-rence	Strokes in		Diffe-rence	Strokes in	
	Singles	Four-somes		Singles	Four-somes		Singles	Four-somes
1	1	0	13	10	5	25	19	9
2	2	1	14	11	5	26	20	10
3	2	1	15	11	6	27	20	10
4	3	2	16	12	6	28	21	11
5	4	2	17	13	6	29	22	11
6	5	2	18	14	7	30	23	11
7	5	3	19	14	7	31	23	12
8	6	3	20	15	8	32	24	12
9	7	3	21	16	8	33	25	12
10	8	4	22	17	8	34	26	13
11	8	4	23	17	9	35	26	13
12	9	5	24	18	9	36	27	14

In Match play strokes received must be taken as under:

STROKES   HOLES

1 at	10																	
2 "	6	12																
3 "	4	10	16															
4 "	4	8	12	16														
5 "	1	5	9	13	17													
6 "	2	5	8	11	14	17												
7 "	1	4	7	10	13	16	18											
8 "	2	4	6	8	10	12	14	16										
9 "	1	3	5	7	9	11	13	15	17									
10 "	1	2	3	5	7	9	11	13	15	17								
11 "	1	2	3	5	7	9	11	13	15	17	18							
12 "	1	3	4	6	7	9	10	12	13	15	16	18						
13 "	2	3	5	6	8	9	10	11	12	14	15	17	18					
14 "	1	2	4	5	6	7	8	10	11	12	13	14	16	17				
15 "	1	2	3	5	6	7	8	9	11	12	13	14	15	17	18			
16 "	1	2	3	4	5	7	8	9	10	11	13	14	15	16	17	18		
17 "	1	2	3	4	5	6	7	8	9	11	12	13	14	15	16	17	18	
18 "	1	2	3	4	5	6	7	8	9	10	11	12	13	14	15	16	17	18

POINTS OF DIFFERENCE BETWEEN THE RULES OF THE ROYAL WIMBLEDON AND ROYAL AND ANCIENT GOLF CLUBS

ROYAL WIMBLEDON GOLF CLUB

RULE 7 – *Ball in Water*
If the ball lie in casual water on the course it may be *teed* behind the hazard, losing one stroke.

If the ball be in water in a hazard, or the water itself be a recognised hazard, it may be lifted and *dropped* behind the hazard, losing one stroke.

ROYAL AND ANCIENT GOLF CLUB

RULE 21
If the ball lie or be lost in water, the player may drop a ball (in the manner described in Rule 19), losing one stroke.

| ROYAL WIMBLEDON GOLF CLUB | ROYAL AND ANCIENT GOLF CLUB |

RULE 9 – *Lost Ball*
If the ball be lost, the player returns to the spot as nearly as possible from which the ball was struck, tees another, and loses one stroke (match or medal play).

RULE 28
If the ball be lost the player's side loses the hole (match play).

RULE 5
Same as RWGC (medal play).

RULE 12 – *Lifting Ball*
In match or medal play a ball may, under a penalty of two strokes, be lifted out of a difficulty of any description, and teed behind the hazard, etc. etc.

RULE 29
In match play a ball must be played wherever it lies (except as otherwise provided), or the hole given up.
In medal play same as RWGC.

RULES 13 AND 30 – *Loose Impediments*
In match play the penalty for removing loose impediments more than a club-length from the ball, when it lies on grass, either on or off the course, is the loss of the hole.
In medal play, loss of two strokes, or disqualification.

RULE 11
Penalty in match or medal play is loss of one stroke.

RULE 16 – *Playing Opponent's Ball*
If a player play the opponent's ball he loses the hole.

RULE 27
A player loses a stroke if he play the opponent's ball.

RULE 20 – *Ball striking Player, etc.*
If by accident the player's ball strike himself or his caddie or clubs, he loses a stroke.

RULE 24
If the player's ball strike or be stopped by himself or his partner, or either of their caddies or clubs, his side loses the hole.

RULE 21 – *Striking Ball twice*
If, in the act of striking, the player strike his ball twice, he loses a stroke.

RULE 24
If, while in the act of playing, the player strike his ball twice, his side loses the hole.
RULE 6
In medal play he loses a stroke.

ROYAL WIMBLEDON GOLF CLUB	ROYAL AND ANCIENT GOLF CLUB
Displacing Opponent's Ball No corresponding rule. (The inference therefore is that it must be submitted to).	RULE 36 If in playing the player's ball displace the opponent's ball, the opponent shall have the option of replacing it.
RULE 25 – *Holing out the Ball* The line to the hole may be pointed out by club shaft only.	RULE 33 The line to the hole may be pointed out, but the person doing so may not touch the ground by hand or club.
No Rule.	RULE 11 In medal play competitors may not discontinue play because of bad weather.
No Rule.	RULE 3 Regulation size of hole 4¼ ins. diameter.

(*Signed*) N. R. FOSTER,
Hon. Sec. R.W.G.C.

CHAPTER TWELVE

Glossary of Technical Terms Frequently Used in Connection with the Game of Golf

Addressing the ball – The act of the player placing himself in position to strike the ball.

Approach – The stroke by which a player endeavours to play his ball on to the putting-green.

Back spin – See *Bottom*.

Baff – To strike the ground immediately behind the ball with the 'sole' of the club-head in playing. The object of so doing is to put undercut on the ball and send it high into the air, to make it fall dead when it lands. See also *Sclaff*.

Baffy-spoon or Baffy – A wooden club with a short shaft and very much lofted in the face, formerly used for playing approaches.

Bent – A coarse grass found on seaside links.

Bogey, Colonel – The meaning of playing against a Bogey score is explained on page 9.

Bone or Horn – A piece of ram's horn, celluloid, wood fibre, or other substance, inserted in the sole of wooden clubs to prevent the face from being injured at the bottom.

Borrow – When a putt requires to be played across sloping ground, the player must borrow, or play the ball a little up the slope to counteract the effect of its falling off down hill while rolling towards the hole.

Bottom – Back-spin, or a spin which will theoretically have the effect of making the ball after alighting roll back towards the player, but which practically only tends to prevent its rolling forward any distance after alighting. Also called 'undercut.'

Brassy – A wooden club shod with brass on the sole.

Break-club – A stone or any other obstacle lying near the ball which might break or injure the club in the act of playing.

Bulger – A club with a convex face.

Bunker – A sand-hole in the golf-course. (I observe from reports of English golf matches that this word is being applied to all hazards, but such is not its original or real meaning.)

Bye – A hole or holes which remain to be played in order to complete the full round of the links, after the match originally agreed upon is finished.

Caddie – The person who carries the golfer's clubs.

Carry – Used to express the distance between the spot from which a ball is driven to the place where it first alights, exclusive of the distance it may thereafter bound or roll. A long carry or a short carry are used to signify the distance a ball must be lofted usually over a hazard.

Cleek – A golf-club with an iron head.

Club – The implement with which the ball is struck in playing golf.

Course – A golf-course is the ground upon which golf is played.

Cup – A small, shallow hole in the course, frequently one made by the stroke of some previous player having removed turf.

Dead – This word is used in two senses: first, when a ball falls without rolling, it is said to fall 'dead'; and second, a ball is said to lie 'dead' when it lies so near the hole that the player is certain to put it in with his next stroke. The term is also applied to putting, and a putt is said to be laid 'dead.'

Divot – A piece of turf. Frequently used to signify a piece of turf cut out of the links in the act of playing a stroke.

Dormy – The condition of a player when he is as many holes ahead of his opponent as there remain holes to be played.

Draw – To play a ball so that it will travel with a curve towards the left hand. (Synonymous with *Hook* and *Pull*.)

Driver or Play-club – The wooden club with which the ball is usually driven from the tee, and with which the ball can be driven the furthest distance.

Driving – Used in two senses: first, playing tee-shots; and second, playing any full strokes.

Duff – To hit the ground behind the ball. With a duffed stroke the ground is hit so far behind that the ball will not be driven any distance; while in a sclaffed stroke, although the ground behind is also struck, the ball will usually be driven nearly as far as if clean hit. See also *Sclaff*.

Face – This word is used in two senses: first, when one speaks of playing a ball over a 'face,' it there signifies the rise of the hazard or ground over which the ball is to be played; second, it is applied to the front part of the club-head which strikes the ball.

Flat – A club is said to be 'flat' when its head is at a very obtuse angle to the shaft.

Fog – Moss; also thick, rank grass.

Follow-through – The continuation of the swing of the club after the ball has been struck.

Foozle – A badly played stroke.

Fore! – The warning cry which a golfer gives to any person apt to be struck by the ball which he has driven or is about to drive.

Fore-caddie – A person employed to go in advance of the players to watch where their balls alight.

Foursome – A golf match in which four persons engage, two playing against the other two.

Globe – Another term for a golf-ball.

Gobble – A putt played with more than necessary force which goes into the hole, such that if the ball had not gone in it would have gone some distance past the hole.

Golf-ball – A ball with which the game of golf is played. See pages 49 et seq.

Grassed – A club is said to be grassed when its face is spooned or sloped back so as to drive the ball high. Only used in connection with wooden clubs.

Green – First, the whole links or golf-course; second, the putting-green or portion of the links devoid of hazards within twenty yards of a hole.

Grip – First, the part of the club shaft grasped by the golfer while playing; second, the grasp itself.

Gutty – A golf-ball made of gutta-percha.

Half-one – When a player gives his opponent 'half-one,' he gives him a handicap of a stroke at every second hole – that is to say, he must, to halve these holes, do each of them in one stroke less than his opponent to whom half-one is conceded.

Half shot – A stroke of less distance than a full shot, and played with a half swing; less than a three-quarter shot and more than a wrist or quarter shot.

Halved – A hole is 'halved' when each side takes the same number of strokes. A match is halved when both sides have won the same number of holes, or have proved equal.

Hanging ball – A hanging ball is one which lies on ground sloping downward in the direction in which it is to be driven.

Hazard – A general term for bunkers, water, sand, loose earth, mole-hills, paths, roads or railways, whins, bushes, rushes, rabbit-scrapes, fences, ditches, or anything which is not the green of the course, except sand blown on to the grass by wind, or sprinkled on grass for preservation of the links, or snow or ice, or bare patches on the course. See Rule 15.

Head – The lowest part of a golf-club.

Heel – First, that part of the club-head nearest the shaft; second, to hit the ball with the heel of the club, which has the effect of driving the ball to the right hand.

Hole – First, the hole in the putting-green into which the ball is played; second, the whole space between any teeing-ground and the actual hole.

Honour – The right to play off first from the tee.

Hook – See *Draw*. Hook on a club refers to the face, when the head is placed flat on the ground, lying in to the ball, and thus having a tendency to 'pull' the strokes.

Horn – See *Bone*.

Hose – The socket of iron-headed clubs into which the shaft is fitted.

Iron – A club with an iron head considerably lofted, to raise the ball.

Jerk – When a stroke is played with a 'jerk' the club-head, after striking the ball, digs into the ground.

Lie – First, the lie of a club refers to the angle of the head to the shaft. A club is said to have a flat lie when the angle is very obtuse, and to have an upright lie when the angle is less. Second, the lie of the ball refers to its position on the links, a good lie signifying that the ball lies clear so that it can easily be struck, and a bad lie signifying that the ball lies in a hole or in heavy grass, etc., and difficult to play.

Lift – To lift a ball is to take it out of a hazard and drop or tee it in conformity with the Rules.

Like – The like is the stroke which equalises the number played by the other side. Thus, after the tee-shots have been driven, the player furthest from the hole plays the 'odds,' and, if he places his ball nearer the hole than his opponent, his opponent then plays the 'like,' and the players (or balls) are said to be 'like as they lie.'

Like as we lie – When both side have played the same number of strokes. See *Like*.

Links – The ground on which golf is played.

Loft – To drive the ball into the air in playing a stroke.

Lofter – A lofting-iron.

Long game – Driving and play through the green.

Long odds – A golfer plays the long odds when he has to play a stroke more than his opponent who is much nearer the hole.

Mashie – An iron club with a deep short blade.

Match – First, the sides playing against each other; second, the game itself.

Match play – Golf played by counting holes lost or won on either side.

Medal play – Golf played by counting the total number of strokes taken to complete the game.

Miss the globe – To fail to strike the ball, as by swinging the club over the top of it, or by hitting the ground behind. This counts a stroke.

Neck – The neck of the club is the bent part of the head where it is connected with the shaft.

Niblick – An iron club with a small, heavy round head, used to play the ball out of bunkers, hazards, and bad lies.

Nose – The nose of the club is the pointed part of the head opposite the neck.

Odds – To play the odds is to play one stroke more than one's opponent.

One off two, one off three, etc. – When your opponent has played three strokes more, your next stroke is 'one off three.' When he has played 'two more' your next stroke is 'one off two,' and so on.

Play-club – See *Driver*.

Press – To strive to hit the ball harder than usual, with the object of getting a longer stroke.

Pull – See *Draw*.

Putt – (The *u* is pronounced as in but). To play strokes near the hole on the putting-green.

Putter – An upright club used for putting.

Putty – A golf-ball made of composition, as opposed to the gutty or gutta-percha ball.

Quarter or wrist shot – A stroke less than a half stroke. Generally played with an iron from the wrists.

Rub of the green – Whatever happens to a ball in motion, such as its being deflected or stopped by any agency outside the match, or by the fore-caddie, is a rub of the green, and the ball must be played from where it lies. See Rule 22.

Run – First, to run the ball along the ground instead of lofting it; second, the run of a drive is the distance the ball runs after alighting on the ground.

Scare – The part of the club where the head and shaft are spliced together.

Sclaff – See *Baff*. The distinction between the two words is somewhat subtle. In baffing a ball the stroke is played with the intention of lofting it high in the air, whereas a sclaffed ball is not necessarily lofted high. See also *Duff*.

Scratch player – One who does not receive any handicap allowance.

Screamer – A very long stroke, so called from the whistling noise made by the ball.

Screw – To put spin on a ball either by 'pulling' or 'slicing' it.

Set of clubs – The complement of clubs carried by a player.

Shaft – The stick or handle of the club.

Short game – Approaching and putting.

Slice – To draw the face of the club across the ball from right to left in the act of hitting it, the result being that it will travel with a curve towards the right.

Socket – The part of the head of iron clubs into which the shaft is fitted.

Sole – The flat bottom part of the club-head which rests on the ground.

Spoons – Clubs having wooden heads, lofted or grassed, so as to loft the ball.

Spring – The degree of suppleness of the club shaft.

Square – Said of a game when it stands level, neither party being any holes ahead.

Stance – The position of the player's feet when addressing himself to the ball.

Steal – To hole a long unlikely putt by a stroke which rolls the ball up to the hole so that it just drops in.

Stroke – Any movement of the club which is intended to strike the ball. See Rule 4.

Stymie – The position of the balls near the hole when one lies directly in the line of putt of the other.

Swing – The mode in which the club is swung when in the act of hitting the ball.

Swipe – A full stroke.

Tee – The elevation, generally a small pinch of sand, on which the ball is placed for the first stroke to each hole.

Teeing-ground – The space marked out within the limits of which the ball must be teed.

Third – A handicap of one stroke allowed at every third hole.

Three-quarter stroke – A stroke of less distance than a full stroke, but more than a half stroke.

Toe – See *Nose*.

Top – To top the ball is to hit it above its centre.

Two more, three more, etc. – To play two more is to play two strokes more than one's opponent. Similarly with three more, etc.

Undercut – To hit the ball, by baffing or otherwise, so that it rises high in the air, and will not, owing to the spin on the ball, roll far after alighting. See *Bottom*.

Upright – See *Lie*.

Whins – Furze or gorse.

Whipping – The twine with which the club head and shaft are bound together.

Wrist shot – See *Quarter shot*.

Index

ards, 117; stance and grip of club, 117; mode of playing ball in bunker, 117; teed ball in a bunker, 118; use wooden club if possible, 119; ball in water, 119; paths and roads, 120; stones, whins, etc., 120; hold club firmly, 121; playing back or to side, 121; individual ingenuity in playing out of, 121; avoiding, 130; position of, 161; repairing bunkers, 167; raking bunkers, 168

Heeling, 79, 142; in wind, 127

Hole, size of, 3; cutting, 166; lining for, 166; flags, 167

Honour, 4; advantage of having the, 129

Honourable the Edinburgh Company of Golfers, 1

Hooking, 69

Interest in Matches, 132

Iron, 13, 15, 18, 23, 29; putting, 13; driving, 13, 21; lofting, 21, 31; niblick, 13, 17, 18, 23, 30, 31; hints as to selecting, 26; shorter swing in playing with iron clubs, 70; effect of pitch on iron clubs, 97

Jerking, 63, 72, 77

Laidlay, Mr J E, position for driving, 55; grip, 58; position for approaching, 96; 'shoulder' shots, 95; position for putting, 107

Laws of golf: Rules of Royal and Ancient Golf Club of St Andrews, with notes, 170; index to St Andrews Rules, 188; additional rules – balls in rabbit holes, etc., 190; players causing undue delay, 191; balls on putting-greens, 191; Rules and Bye-Laws of Royal Wimbledon Golf Club, 191; table of match-play odds, 202; points of difference between St Andrews and Wimbledon Rules, 203

Laying out and keeping golf-links, 155; suitable ground for links, 155, 156; number of holes, 157; older golf-courses, 156; necessity for experienced assistance in laying out links, 156; position of holes, 157; shape of links, 158; length of holes, 158; position of tees, 160; position of putting-greens, 161; position and character of hazards, 161; traps, 161; blind holes, 163; clearing ground, 163; repairing links, 164; changing round, 164; materials for repairs, 164; top-dressing putting-greens, 165; rolling and cutting, 165; cutting hole, 166; flags, 167; marking teeing-grounds, 167; repairing bunkers, 167; grazing, 168; walking over links, 168

Learning golf, best way to employ coach, 124; practising different strokes, 124; watching play of good golfer, 125; improvement, 125

Leather faces in clubs, 22

Left-handed golfers, 32

Length of drives, 71

—of holes, 187; on St Andrews Links, 187

Leven Links, 3

Links, 2, 3; laying out and keeping. See Laying out, etc.; extent and form of, 2

Lofting-iron, 21, 28, 30

Long game, 71

Red Coats, 37

Roads. *See* Hazards.

Royal and Ancient Golf Club, Play at Autumn Meeting of 1893, 135

Royal Musselburgh Golf Club, 1

Rules of Golf, *See* Laws.

—necessity for knowing, 130

St Andrews Caddies, 139

—Links, 3, 164; length of holes, 187

Sandwich Links, 3

Sclaffing, 80

Set of golf-clubs, 23

Shafts, club, 23

Shoulder shots, 95

Single, 4

Slicing, 69, 78, 79; in putting, 110

Snow, 34

Spoons, 13, 14, 19, 26, 30; brassy, 15, 19; baffy, 19; hints as to selecting, 27

Stance, for driving, 48; position must be easy, 48; rules for, 51; hard and fast lines cannot be laid down, 52; advancing right of left foot, 52; position of ball, 54; Mr Laidlay's position, 55; freedom in taking up stance, 56; variations on stance for approaching and putting, 56; stance in long game, 73; in approaching, 86; Mr Laidlay's stance for approaches, 95; stance for putting, 105; Mr Laidlay's stance for putting, 107; stance in bunkers, 117

Stones. *See* Hazards.

Straight play, advantage of, 125

Style of play, 39

Stymies, 111; modes of playing, 112; should not be played unless to secure half of hole, 112

Swing; 56; ball should be swept away, 58; desirability of long swing, 58; too long a swing, 58; position of body before swing, 58; Mr Laidlay's position, 58; upward part of swing, 58; body should pivot round backbone, 59; downward part of swing, 60; follow-through, 60; undesirable and desirable kinds of swing, 62; swaying body, 63; upward and downward swings one motion, 63; jerking swing, 63; putting force into swing, 63; getting wrists into stroke, 66; 'slow back' condemned, 66; bending body from waist, 66; moving feet during swing, 66; swings round head, shoulders, and body, 68; effects of, 68; danger of too upright a swing, 68; club should not touch body, 68; 'whipping up' the ball, 68; slicing, 69; pulling and hooking, 69; face of club should not be hung over ball, 69; waggle, 69; ball should be hit with centre of club face, 70; falling forward on ball, 70; shorter swing in playing iron clubs, 70; 'keep your eye on the ball,' 70; summary of actions in playing, 70

Tait, Mr F G, 135

Taylor, J H, grip of club, 55

Technical terms, glossary of, 207

Teeing-grounds, 3; position of, 160; marking, 167

Tees; selection of, 72; high tee, 73; low tee against a head wind, 73; mode of making, 73; good and bad, 73; club touching ground behind, 73; removing obstructions, etc., 73; hints as to teeing,

Some other books published by **LUATH** PRESS

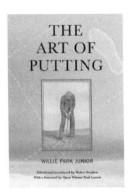

The Art of Putting
Willie Park Junior
ISBN 1 905222 66 1
PBK £5.99

In these few pages is, after all, the wisdom of a lifetime, the wisdom of the best putter of his time.
PAUL LAWRIE

'Putting is the key to success in golf. The man who can Putt is a match for anyone.' So said Willie Park in 1920. It is still true today.

Where should you place your feet?
How should you grip the club?
What type of ball is best?

Willie Park's transcendent manual seeks to share the methods which made him 'the best and most consistent putter in the world'. Equipment may have changed and competition become fiercer, but with Park's guidance, you too will have a fighting chance of making that all-important putt.

This guide to putting for players of all skill levels
• is fully illustrated.
• covers every aspect of putting, from grip to the lie of the green.
• is a clear, concise and detailed guide to mastery of technique.

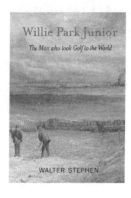

Willie Park Junior: The Man Who Took Golf To The World
Walter Stephen
ISBN 1 905222 21 1
HBK £25.00

A book that is quirky, idiosyncratic, frustrating and ultimately as fascinating as the game itself.
THE HERALD

In the 19th century, Musselburgh, Scotland was a hotbed of golfing genius. The local links produced five Open Champions, and of these golfing greats, Willie Park Junior was undoubtedly more than just a good golfer. Park redefined the image of the golf professional and took the game from being an esoteric pastime, practised in a few favoured localities, to its present status as a worldwide game.

A two-time winner of the Open, Park also played challenge and demonstration matches at home and abroad. Ever the entrepreneur, his workshops turned out golf balls and clubs to his own design, with retail outlets in Edinburgh, Manchester, London, New York and Montreal, and Park was the first golf professional to write a manual – *The Game of Golf* – which appeared in 1896. His career in golf course design took him from Britain to Western Europe and then North America; in total Park lay out over 160 courses worldwide, over 40 of these in the United States and more than 20 in Canada, many of which are still in use today.

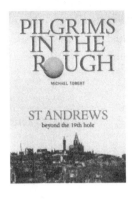

Pilgrims in the Rough: St Andrews beyond the 19th Hole
Michael Tobert
ISBN 0 946487 74 X
PBK £7.99

An extraordinary book.
THE OBSERVER

With ghosts, witches and squabbling clerics, *Pilgrims in the Rough* is a funny and affectionate portrayal of Michael Tobert's home town. The author has always wanted to write a travel book – but he has done more than that. Combining tourist information with history, humour and anecdote, he has written a book that will appeal to golfer and non golfer, local and visitor, alike.

While *Pilgrims in the Rough* is more than just a guide to clubs and caddies, it is nonetheless packed with information for the golf enthusiast. It features a detailed map of the course and the low down from a regular St Andrews player on booking times, the clubs and each of the holes on the notorious Old Course. The book also contains an informative guide to the attractions of the town and the best places to stay and to eat out. Michael Tobert's infectious enthusiasm for St Andrews will even persuade the most jaded golf widow or widower that the town is worth a visit!

Luath Press Limited

committed to publishing well written books worth reading

LUATH PRESS takes its name from Robert Burns, whose little collie
Luath (*Gael.*, swift or nimble) tripped up Jean Armour at a wedding
and gave him the chance to speak to the woman who was to be his
wife and the abiding love of his life. Burns called one of 'The Twa
Dogs' Luath after Cuchullin's hunting dog in Ossian's
Fingal. Luath Press was established in 1981 in the heart of
Burns country, and is now based a few steps up the road
from Burns' first lodgings on Edinburgh's Royal Mile.
Luath offers you distinctive writing with a hint of unex-
pected pleasures. Most bookshops in the UK, the US,
Canada, Australia, New Zealand and parts of Europe,
either carry our books in stock or can order them for you.
To order direct from us, please send a £sterling cheque,
postal order, international money order or your credit card
details (number, address of cardholder and expiry date) to
us at the address below. Please add post and packing as follows: UK
– £1.00 per delivery address; overseas surface mail – £2.50 per delivery address; overseas airmail – £3.50 for the first book to each delivery address, plus £1.00 for each additional book by airmail to the
same address. If your order is a gift, we will happily enclose your
card or message at no extra charge.

ILLUSTRATION: IAN KELLAS

Luath Press Limited
543/2 Castlehill
The Royal Mile
Edinburgh EH1 2ND
Scotland
Telephone: 0131 225 4326 (24 hours)
Fax: 0131 225 4324
email: sales@luath.co.uk
Website: www.luath.co.uk